WAY TO GO

An Illustrated History of Transportation

Chris Chant and John Batchelor

LONGMEADOW
PRESS

Published by Longmeadow Press, 201 High Ridge Road, Stamford, CT 06904.

Cover design by Graham Beehag
Interior design by Graham Beehag

Library of Congress Catologing-in-Publication Data
ISBN 0-681-10434-1

Printed in Italy

Edition
0 9 8 7 6 5 4 3 2 1

Contents

Land Transportation

Sea Transportation

Air Transportation

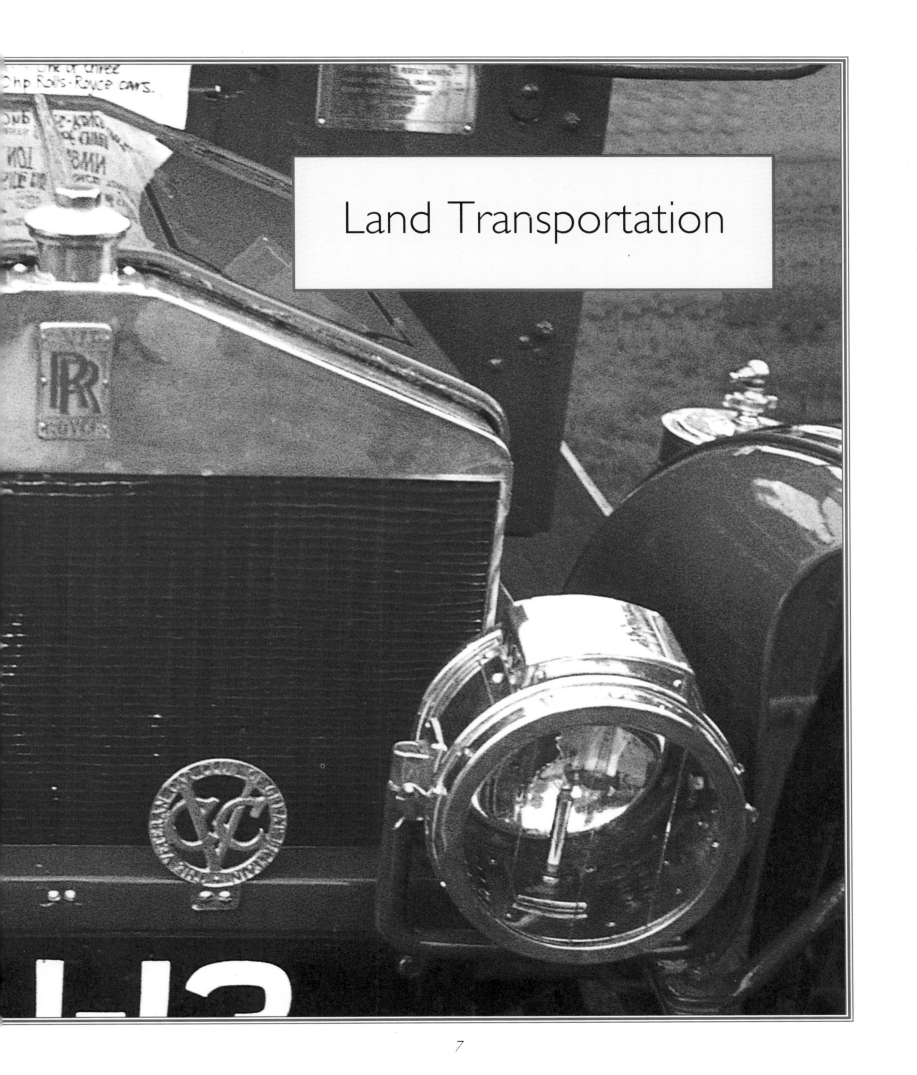

Land Transportation

Locomotives

When the United States secured its independence from the British in 1783, the 13 ex-colonies occupied the eastern seaboard of the North American continent as far south as Florida. It was still a comparatively new land, and a land of plenty. But this plenty had been developed mostly in terms of agriculture and trade. Yet the beginnings of the country's future greatness were already apparent, and fledgling industry was appearing to capitalize on the deposits of coal and iron ore that had already been discovered. To this extent, therefore, the need for ways of moving heavy loads was already appreciated, and these emergent American industries were not far behind their European counterparts in applying existing concepts, while exploring new technologies to ease a problem that could only become more acute as industries developed. Wagonways of the European pattern were already in service for mining purposes, and development of steam power was in hand. But starting from a smaller industrial base some 3,000 miles removed from the powerhouse of Great Britain, this process was inevitably slow.

In these circumstances it was inevitable that the first and greatest strides had already been made on the other side of the Atlantic.

The most telling example of these strides was the steam locomotive.

If the horse and wagon saw the start of the Industrial Revolution in the USA and then the opening of the West, it was the steam locomotive and, to a lesser extent, the steam paddlewheeler that made possible their full development and exploitation, as two of the cornerstones of the USA's development into a large and modern state.

Richard Trevithick's steam locomotive was a workable, but hardly practical, machine that nevertheless presaged the emergence of a new form of land transport that was soon developed into a major force in the development of the modern world.

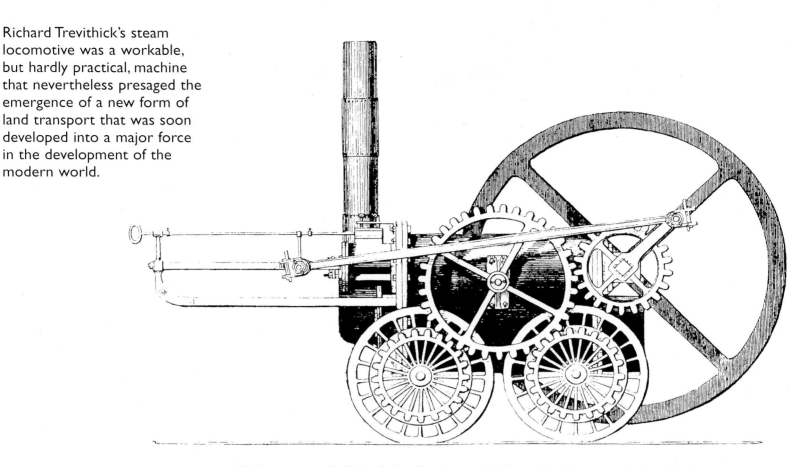

This was a child of the Industrial Revolution, and also helped to make this revolution the world-shattering force that it became. As is often the case with movements that rapidly become huge forces for change in the world, it is difficult to put a precise date on the beginning of the Industrial Revolution, but it is fair to say that, by about 1760 in Great Britain, the combination of scientific and technological development, the availability of raw materials such as iron and coal, and the entrepreneurial spirit were such that the Industrial Revolution was inevitable. Thus, the reign of King George III (1760-1820) may be taken as the beginning of the revolution that turned Britain from a country relying mainly on agriculture and trade for its livelihood, into a country that based its living on the manufacture and export of goods.

In any such country, the swift and economical inward delivery of raw materials to the factories, and the steady outward shipment of finished goods to major cities and ports are both essential. Canals certainly played their part in the inward movement of bulk freight such as coal and iron to the factories, but canal traffic was too slow and roundabout for the outward movement of finished goods, which needed to reach more destinations than could be served by the geographically limited canal network, even when aided by horse-drawn wagons. Another factor of the Industrial Revolution that helped the invention and development of railroads was the alteration of the British population pattern. Manufacturing industries had to be highly concentrated, leading to the rapid growth of the population of

Early railroads invested enormous sums of money in creating their route infrastructure. Construction projects such as this cutting near Olive Mount were undertaken so that as a direct a line as possible could be created.

industrial cities: these new urban populations could not, of course, produce their own food, and their demand for supplies could only be met by the timely arrival of fresh produce from the surrounding countryside. The cities continued to grow as the Industrial Revolution gathered pace, so the area from which food had to be shipped increased to the extent that only railroads could supply the right quantities in the time before the food rotted.

The single factor that allowed the development of a successful railroad network in Great Britain was steam power, itself both a child of the early Industrial Revolution and a parent of the

This is the London and Birmingham Railway Company's No. 1 locomotive designed by Edward Buss, who was the only significant competitor to the Stephensons as a locomotive designer in the 1830s.

This is a Robert Stephenson locomotive of the 1840s. The machine is a long-boiler type with a 4-2-0 wheel arrangement with four small and unpowered front wheels, two large and powered main wheels, and no rear wheels.

later Industrial Revolution. Yet the 'railroad concept' was much older than the Industrial Revolution itself. As early as the beginning of the 16th century, for example, German coal miners had found that it was easier to move heavy loads of coal if the cartwheels ran on smooth tracks. The solution was to lay parallel tracks of wooden planks over the rough ground and push the carts along these tracks. The inevitable problem was how to prevent the carts, with their flat-rimmed wheels from wandering of the tracks: the solution evolved by the middle of the 15th century in places such as Leberthal in Alsace was the railed cart and, by the middle of the 18th century, this had been developed into a system of flanged metal wheels running on iron rails. This improved the overall capability of the system to the extent that horses could be used to haul the carts, which were soon developed into wagons with the capacity for even heavier loads.

By the beginning of the 19th century, steam was well established as the power source driving the Industrial Revolution. These early steam engines were not notably efficient and were very heavy. Even so, far-sighted inventors were already at work trying to develop a steam-powered form of transport. Two of the earliest pioneers were James Watt and William Murdoch, who sought to exploit steam power in the creation of a mechanical road carriage. Less farsighted, but eminently more practical, was Richard Trevithick, who appreciated that the best way to harness the power of existing steam engines was in a locomotive for use on a wagonway. To Trevithick falls the distinction of having built the world's first practical steam locomotive, which first ran at Coalbrookdale in Shropshire in 1803 and which, on its

Modesty had never been one of the becoming virtues of the advertising industry, and this was as true in the 19th century as it is today. Steam power was so important to the development of industry and communications in the 19th century that considerable ingenuity and hyperbole went into the advertising of steam engines, as revealed by this beautifully executed advertisement for the wares of the American Machine Works located in Springfield, Massachusetts. The company offered fuel-economical engines designed by Philos B Tyler in power ratings between 3 and 400 hp, and of the high- or low-pressure types with all the latest features – a type of advertisement that presaged the inducements to buy today's automobiles!

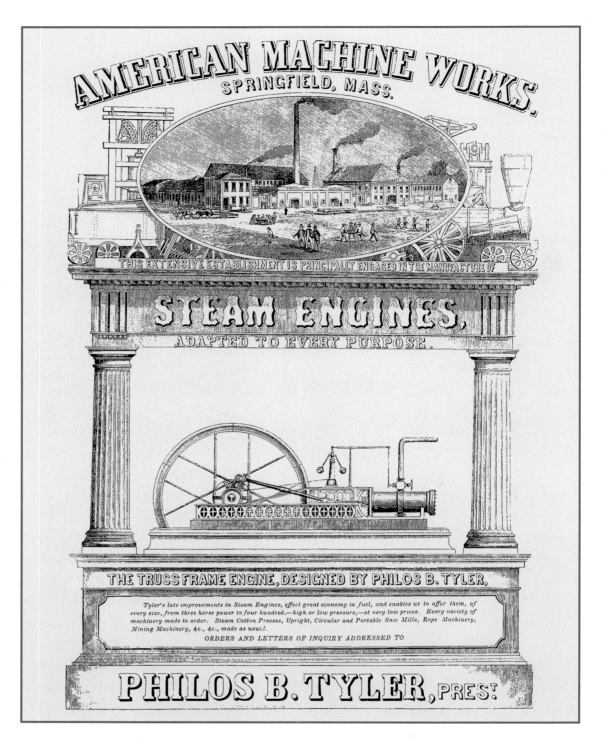

trial runs during 1804, proved itself able to haul wagons carrying 15 tons of iron, at the Pen-y-Darren ironworks in South Wales. Trevithick's development was to a certain extent a dead end, for there was immense hostility against the primitive railroad by ironworkers, who feared the loss of their jobs if horses were replaced by steam locomotives, and the wagonway itself was not strong enough to carry the weight of the locomotive without breaking frequently.

The South Wales iron industry may have rejected the steam locomotive, but the coal industry of northeast England was more perceptive. In 1812, the Middleton Colliery Railway (established by an act of Parliament in 1758) started to use the world's first commercial steam locomotive, designed by Matthew Murray; by 1820, steam

Believed to be the oldest photograph of a working steam engine, this picture shows William Hedley's *Puffing Billy*. This locomotive was built in 1813 for the tramway near Newcastle in Northumberland of the Wylam colliery, where Hedley was superintendent. It was the first locomotive to be built with more than one powered axle. Hedley achieved this feat by the use of gears, and the result gave considerably more tractive power for the movement of larger quantities of coal, and for the ability to tackle more acute gradients.

locomotives designed by Timothy Hackworth, William Hedley, and George Stephenson were in service on the comparatively steep wagonways of the coal mines, at which these men were the chief engineers. But these were private 'rail roads' designed solely for the movement of coal and some of the heavy equipment at the mines. Considerable design, manufacturing, and operating experience had been gained, however, and this proved invaluable when the world's first public steam railroad was planned. The spur for this development was the need of local businessmen to move coal from the mines in the south of County Durham to the port of Stockton on the River Tees. The local consortium appointed the self-taught Stephenson as the chief engineer of its Stockton & Darlington Railway. Stephenson designed and supervised the construction of the track, and designed and built the pioneering steam locomotive Locomotion, which, on September 27, 1825, opened the line by hauling a load of 68 tons along the 21-mile track from Shildon to Stockton. There was enormous enthusiasm for the overall concept, but people did not altogether trust the concept of steam locomotion. In its first eight years of operation, the Stockton & Darlington Railway moved only coal and goods under steam power; people were still moved in horse-drawn carriages.

Even so, the commercial advantages of steam locomotion were soon clear as the railroad began to provide a handsome profit for its owners, and this success encouraged the development of other British railroads and spread the idea to other countries. In 1827, the first

Stephenson's Rocket

In 1813 the British pioneer William Hedley made the *Puffing Billy* steam engine with two upright cylinders at the rear of the boiler, one on each side. The pistons moving in these cylinders operated beams which transmitted the motion to four road wheels by means of long connecting pods, cranks and toothed wheels. The waste steam was passed up a chimney at the front of the boiler, and this produced a puff of steam at each stroke of the system.

It was from the *Puffing Billy*'s concept that George Stephenson developed the more sophisticated concept for his own locomotives. The first of these appeared in 1814, and led the way to the *Rocket* that appeared in 1829. The *Rocket* had two cylinders, one on each side of the boiler and pointing at the axle of the front pair of wheels. The pistons worked connecting rods attached to pins on the spokes of the driving wheels.

Thus far the *Rocket* was typical of its period, and its success lay with its tubular boiler rather than mechanical system. The boiler contained 25 3-inch copper tubes that transmitted the heat of the fire-box at the rear evenly through the boiler to the funnel at the front. It was this boiler's steam pressure, which was high and sustained for the period, that allowed the *Rocket* to achieve a maximum speed of 29 mph, and an average speed of 12.5 mph in the Darlington trials conducted in 1929. These trials were held to find the right locomotive for the Liverpool and Manchester Railway. After the success of the *Rocket*, Stephenson was asked to built railroads and locomotives in other parts of the UK, and he always said: "*Make [the railroads] all the same width; they may be a long way off now, but some day they will be joined together.*" It was a far-sighted prophecy, for within a few years the UK had 6,600 miles of railroad track that increased to 20,000 miles by 1890.

Right: The coming of the railroad effected a major change in the nature of urban and rural areas alike in the 19th century. The railroad tracks demanded gentle curves and comparatively small gradients. Thus the transformation of industrialized countries by the creation of the railroads was akin to the changes wrought by the introduction of the canal system at an earlier date, but was ultimately far more extensive. Cuttings were driven through hills and embankments were created to produce the combination of curves and gradients that could be handled by the steam locomotives of the period. Here an early, and typically smoky, locomotive tows its string of carriages over a carefully constructed embankment.

Austrian railroad was built, and in the same year, the first portion of the Baltimore & Ohio Railroad was opened. The first French railroad followed the next year, and within 10 years railroads were beginning to appear all over Europe, as well as in most parts of the USA and other more advanced countries. In the UK, the railroads first resulted from the Industrial Revolution and spurred its advance, but the railroads generally preceded the birth of the Industrial Revolution in other countries. The building of these other railroads linked major centers first, and then encouraged the growth of new industrial centers along their routes.

These early railroads were designed principally for the movement of goods, and their use for passenger transport was an incidental one,

It is believed that the figure standing by the *Rocket*'s tender, used for the carriage of fuel and spare boiler water, is Robert Stephenson, the designer of this celebrated and epoch-making locomotive. The locomotive was designed for the Liverpool and Manchester Railway, which sold the engine in 1839 to the owner of a colliery in Carlisle. In 1851 this second owner gave the famous engine to the Robert Stephenson works for preservation as a historical monument.

though profitable. The first railroad planned for the movement of goods and people was the Liverpool & Manchester Railway: the cities had each more than doubled in population since 1790, were fairly close to each other on a flat stretch beside the River Mersey, and were a major port and a major manufacturing center respectively. The capable Stephenson was again made chief engineer, and while he reserved his energies for the creation of the track (with its several bridges and tunnels), he appointed his son Robert to undertake the creation of the locomotive. The family did not have things entirely its own way, however, for Robert Stephenson's design, the Rocket, was selected for the Liverpool & Manchester Railway only after evaluation against other pioneering steam locomotives in the 1829 Rainhill Trials.

The first regular passenger run by a train with a steam locomotive was a one-mile stretch between Bogshole Farm and South Street on the rail route between Canterbury and Whitstable, Kent, in southeast England. The locomotive Invicta was used on this route, which opened for passenger traffic on May 30, 1830. But this section is too short for consideration as the world's first properly constituted passenger operation by rail, which must therefore be attributed to the Liverpool & Manchester Railway's service, which began with a tragic accident on September 15, 1830: one of the guests at the formal opening, the politician William Huskisson, stumbled as he crossed the track and was killed by the Rocket. The accident failed to have any significant impact on public opinion, and within a few weeks, the railroad was carrying twice as many passengers as the stagecoaches had carried between the same two destinations before the opening of the railroad. By the end of the year, half the stagecoach operators had been forced out of business.

In the following years, genuine goods and passenger railroads blossomed all over the UK, and the pattern established in the UK was followed, initially to a smaller extent and with modification for the fact that it was leading rather than following the development of the Industrial Revolution, in Europe, North America, and other parts of

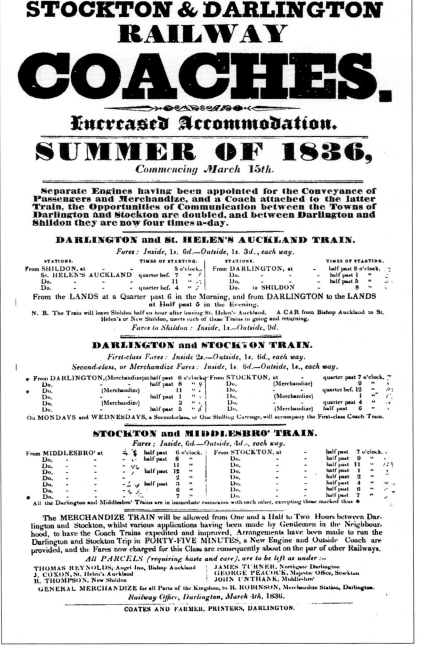

The Stockton and Darlington Railway company began to operate in 1825 and managed to maintain its commercial independence up to 1863, when it was brought into the railroad empire of the North Eastern company. As the pioneer of railroad passenger services, the Stockton and Darlington company had begun with very limited capability (one a single service, in fact), but had then expanded into a number of related services with interior or exterior accommodation.

the world. The stagecoach operators suffered proportionately, but canals continued to be the cheapest way of moving bulk cargoes that did not need rapid delivery. By 1851, the British could travel by rail from their capital in London to the major provincial centers such as Birmingham, Bristol, Liverpool, Manchester, and Southampton, and the beginnings of a railroad network were appearing in Scotland, which was linked to England by main rail lines from Edinburgh and Glasgow.

Wherever railroads sprang up, they brought a change in people's ways of life. One of their first results was the rapid explosion of manufacturing industries, which led to the growth of the 'leisure industry' as people sought to escape from their grim workplaces and homes into the surrounding countryside, and even to the seaside for weekends and vacations. The creation of the famous coastal resorts in the U.K. would have been impossible without railroads. Rail travel was fairly cheap, allowing families who had migrated from depressed rural areas to the more wealthy cities to keep in touch with their families, either by direct travel or by the improving postal services made possible by rail transport. Standards of comfort varied widely: first-class passengers were seated in covered passenger cars, second-class passengers were seated in open cars, and third-class passengers stood in cars with open sides. As rail travel matured, however, improved conditions became standard, and even third-class passengers were provided with basic seating in covered cars.

Right into the second half of the 19th century, British steam locomotives, engineers, and even 'navvies' (inland navigators) led the way in the development of the European rail network. Only Scandinavia had yet to move into the railroad age. But as the railroad concept gained ground and economic importance, various European countries began to develop their own railroad industries, and the British – in an effort to maintain their domestic industry – exported skills and equipment to their empire, and to nations such as China and Egypt, and to the developing countries of South and Central America.

From about 1850, however, the USA began to emerge as the real giant of railroad construction. This was little appreciated at the time, for the American effort was devoted largely to domestic development. Considerable trouble was encountered by the American railroad pioneers. There was jealous financial opposition from the canal and stagecoach operators, and there was also considerable opposition from churchmen opposed to any form of steam power. These objections were eventually swept aside, and by 1850, the eastern side of the United States was well served by the railroad network running from the Canadian frontier to the Gulf of Mexico.

The pace of technical development in the early days of commercial railroads was fast and furious as the designers of locomotives refined their concepts to produce engines offering greater power at a reduced rate of consumption of fuel and water. Thus it came to be that operation of the latest equipment was one of the only ways to retain commercial parity with competitors. This is a German Class D locomotive of 1856. It is possible to see in this engine how, in just over a quarter of a century, from the creation of the *Rocket,* the science of steam power transformed the locomotive from a primitive machine into a relatively sophisticated one offering not only greater power, but also considerably improved reliability.

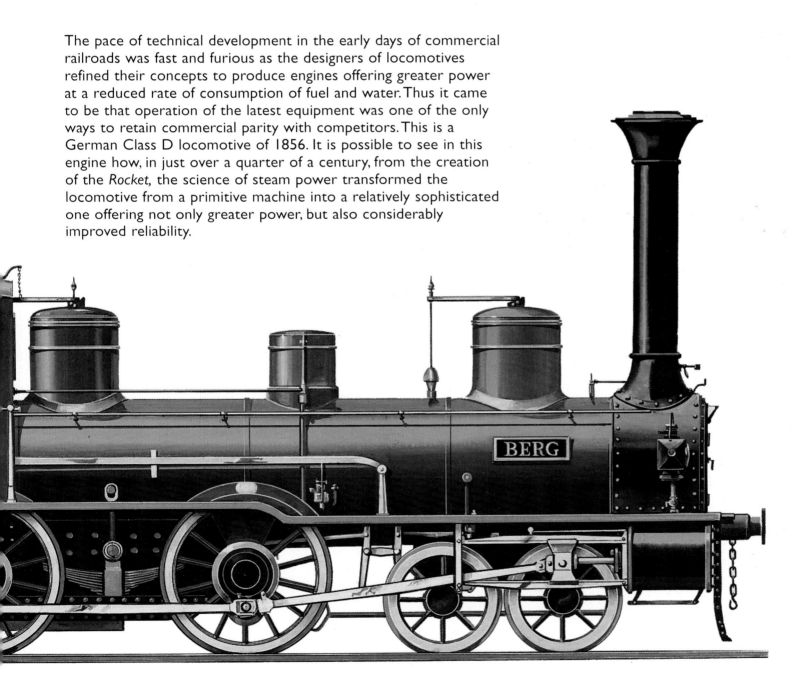

Above left: This is an American Jupiter class 4-4-0 locomotive of the 1860s complete with a large front-mounted device to move any animals or other obstructions off the line before it can damage or derail the locomotive.

Above: This is another 4-4-0 locomotive of the 1860s used on the American railroad system.

Left: A legacy of an earlier generation of American steam locomotives, this is a Lafayette class 4-2-0 locomotive of the 1830s.

Below: The growing network of railroad systems in the more populated parts of the industrialized world, soon attracted the attentions of governments and armies alike. The former saw the development of their countries' railways as a vital ingredient of economic development, and the latter as the means of moving large numbers of men and equipment over strategic distances without the problems associated with road transport.

Above: The steam locomotives designed from the last quarter of the 19th century had reached something of a technical plateau, but differed considerably in the details of their design such as the wheel layout. This is a 2-8-0 locomotive of the D & RG railroadís narrow-gauge line in the 1880s.

Above right: Freight, generally in the form of domestic goods on the outward trip and animals and/or animal products, was a staple of the American railroad industry in the mid-West and West during the later part of the 19th century. This is a 4-4-0 locomotive pulling typical freight cars.

Right: Older locomotives still retained a commercial value well into the present century for purposes that emphasized load-pulling capability, reliability and economy. This is an 18-ton Shay locomotive in use on Vancouver Island in 1962.

Built in India, this 0-4-2 narrow-gauge locomotive was used by the Burma States Railway.

This Atlantic class 4-4-2 steam locomotive was used to pull commuter services as recently as 1954 in the USA.

One of the driving forces behind the development of the American rail network was the need to expand westward through the mountain ranges that had kept industry pinned in the eastern one-fifth of the country: roads could be driven through these mountains to help the westward surge, but canals clearly could not, and the railroad companies emphasized that wherever roads went, railroads could be pushed through to allow the carriage of far greater numbers of people and quantities of freight. Under the weight of this argument,

Steam locomotives have survived longer in the third-world than in more industrialized countries, and still have a considerable part to play in the local economy of countries such as Indonesia, where this 0-10-0 locomotive is operated on the island of Sumatra.

The notion of the steam locomotive still exerts a powerful attraction over many people, and this is largely responsible for the preservation of many fine examples of such engines in working order or, as in this case, in the Railroad Museum of Sacramento in California.

opposition to the railroads began to crumble, especially when the social and financial advantages of railroad expansion became clear. The huge scale of the American effort is revealed by the fact that, by 1850, the US railroad companies were laying as much track as the rest of the world combined.

Throughout this period, the technological development of the Industrial Revolution had been matched by improved steam locomotives. Better understanding of the physical processes involved in the generation of steam, and its use to work the pistons that drove the locomotive's wheels, allowed more efficient use of the steam: this allowed greater loads to be pulled using less steam, allowing longer distances to be covered before it became essential to refill the boiler

This 4-4-0 engine of the New York and Central was the first steam locomotive to exceed 100 mph, and is now an exhibition item.

This French 4-6-0 locomotive was built in 1905 and used on the prestige route between Paris and Orleans.

This is a 4-6-0 steam locomotive of the Russian imperial railroad system of 1910, a time when Tsarist Russia was making great effort to transform itself into a modern industrial state without changing the nature of its political system which was based on the complete autocracy of the Tsar.

with water and replenish the coal. Greater understanding of metallurgy allowed better materials to be used in the construction of steam locomotives, and improved methods of casting and machining metal allowed the moving parts of the locomotive to be formed with greater precision, promoting greater efficiency. The suspension of the locomotive and carriages was improved, and in combination with greater skill in the planning of routes and laying of tracks, higher speeds and improved traveling comfort were possible.

Most European nations saw the railroads as a basic part of their national lives for military as well as the more obvious economic and social reasons. Consequently, the nations of mainland Europe moved early to the position in which their governments took an active part in the development and running of railroads, either indirectly through the payment of subsidies to operators (the policy generally adopted in the second half of the 19th century), or directly through the takeover of railroad companies to create national railroad networks (the policy that was followed increasingly in the 20th century).

In the USA and the UK, however, it was not the policy of governments to become involved with railroads, except for the granting of licenses to build. Yet railroads were so profitable in the middle of the 19th century that businessmen and financiers seemed insatiable in their appetites to 'get into' the railroad business. In the UK, the years between 1845 and 1847 saw a 'railway mania,' and in 1846 at least 815 private railroad schemes were offered to Parliament for approval! Many were impossible dreams, but the industry employed 250,000 men by the end of the 1840s,

By the beginning of the 20th century, railroad engineering had reached a very high level of technical expertise. This is a French locomotive of 1911, a 4-6-4 type with a four-cylinder compound engine, designed to make possible the operation of long routes at a consistently high speed.

and perhaps one-tenth of the nation's wealth was tied up in railroad building.

The same situation held sway in the United States. The UK had seen its 'railway kings' come and go, but in the far bigger USA. the lords of the railroads were the 'railroad barons' such as Cornelius Vanderbilt, head of the New York Central Railroad. By the end of the 19th century, Vanderbilt's empire covered about 10,000 route miles (16,000 km), and the attitude of the 'railroad barons' is revealed by Vanderbilt's famous exclamation, "Law! What do I care about Law! Ain't I got the power?"

And truly, such men did have power. Their railroads made the USA into a unified country that was rapidly able to develop its huge interior, so that beef and grain could be moved into the industrial cities such as Chicago, Cincinnati, Cleveland, Detroit, Philadelphia, and Pittsburgh, which soon became the massive industrial heart of a nation whose goods were exported through ports such as Baltimore and New York.

The railroads also crossed the country from coast to coast, and so brought California, Oregon, and Washington firmly into social and economic unity with the rest of the country. The first such link came with the completion of the Union Pacific Railroad's trans-American route in May 1869, and another four railroad links soon followed. Similar progress was achieved in other countries and continents. Three years earlier, the first trans-Canadian rail link had been completed by Canadian Pacific. In Europe, a spate of tunnel-building transformed international rail links: the 1853 opening of the Semmering tunnel linked Austria and Hungary, the two major

The British railroad lines competed strongly in terms of speeds and other parameters, a rival engine from the Great Western being this 4-6-0 locomotive *Caerphilly Castle*.

adjuncts of the Austro-Hungarian Empire; in 1871, the opening of the Mont Cenis tunnel allowed the completion of the rail link between France and Italy; and in 1886, the completion of the St. Gotthard tunnel linked Switzerland and Italy.

Until 1850, the UK, northern France, the Low Countries, the German states, and the core of Austria-Hungary were the only areas with what can be called a true railroad network, though other regions and countries had smaller railroads linking main urban and/or industrial centers. Between 1850 and 1870, however, there was a real explosion of railroad communications, so that Spain, southern and western France, Italy, Switzerland, much of Austria-Hungary,

Above: This is an Italian 4-6-2 locomotive of the national railroad company, in 1928.

Ireland, Scandinavia, and even western Russia joined the European rail community. The process continued between 1870 and the outbreak of World War I. The countries of Europe which gained a railroad network or expanded a limited network in this period were Portugal, Spain, the rest of Austria-Hungary, Serbia, Bulgaria, Romania, and

This Warrior class 0-6-0 locomotive is pulling a load of coal wagons from Bickershaw colliery in the UK, where steam locomotives saw some of their last use in this type of mundane but all-important commercial task.

A steam locomotive pulls out from the station of Kuala Lumpur, the capital of the state of Malaysia, and in the process provides a contrast between the different influences of the West and the spiritual world of Islam.

Locomotive No.45562 is seen here at the yards of Normanton in the county of Yorkshire.

The *Duchess of Hamilton* is seen on departure from York station in the county of Yorkshire.

Sir Nigel Gresley, a very nicely streamlined steam locomotive designed and built for one of the prestige long-distance routes of the British railroad system, before the advent of diesel and electric locomotives rendered it obsolescent. It is now used to pull the Cumbrian Mountain Express.

The *Earl,* a light locomotive of the Llanfair Railway, crosses a river bridge in the course of earning its daily, or at least seasonal, crust as part of a preserved railroad route.

Preserved at Amberawa on the Indonesian island of Java, this is a rack locomotive used for special routes with a gradient too steep for conventional locomotives.

the whole of western Russia, including Finland, Poland, and the Caucasus.

The size of locomotives, as well as their performance in terms of speed and tractive power, continued to increase during this period, which is the heyday of steam railroads. Locomotives were the primary means of moving large numbers of passengers or major loads of freight over long distances. And, as route mileage and tonnage

The *Pendennis Castle* of the Great Western Railway emerges from the Winchcombe tunnel during the course of an excursion run.

Above: The final stages in the development of the steam locomotive saw the design and construction of some exceptional engines, characterized by great power and very good streamlining for use on long-distance routes at sustained high speeds. Typical of this breed was this 4-8-4 locomotive of the Southern Pacific Railroad.

Right: Modern locomotives may have lost the nostalgic appeal of steam power, but there are still mechanically magnificent machines being built, such as this EMD F-45 *Warbonnet* pictured in 1990.

increased, greater effort was made to appeal to the traveling customers' desire for comfort. Until about 1860, few trains had anything but primitive seating except in the first-class carriages. Washroom and refreshment facilities were non-existent; heating was provided by a coal-burning stove, and light by smoking oil lamps. Such conditions were acceptable on short journeys, but for longer (and overnight) trips, which became increasingly common after 1860, better facilities were important, as the more far-sighted were swift to appreciate, bet-

Far left: It was the advent of the fully developed steam locomotive that made the development of practical long-distance travel for anyone other than the very rich possible, as suggested by this poster for the London & South Western Railway.

Left: One of the most celebrated railroad services in the world is the Orient Express, linking Paris and Istanbul, the capitals of France and Turkey. This poster of the Companie des Wagons Lits emphasizes the comfort and social propriety of the service in conjunction with the Golden Arrow service that allowed passengers to reach Paris from London and so link with the Orient Express, in a combined service that made a comfortable, and indeed glamorous, railroad trip from London to Istanbul.

ter conditions encourage more customers, who would be prepared to pay a premium for greater comfort.

First off the mark was an American, George Pullman, who by 1865 had persuaded some American railroads that overnight journeys should have sleeper accommodation. Pullman built sleeping cars, which were attached to a railroad's trains: the railroads pocketed the basic fare, and Pullman made his profit by charging a premium to passengers using the sleeper accommodation. This was only the beginning, and Pullman rapidly developed his idea, initially including a small kitchen so that passengers could order meals, and later intro-

With abundant oil supplies and an advanced automotive industry, its is hardly surprising that the USA was one of the first into the field of diesel-powered locomotives such as this EMD E-5A unit, able to cruise at high speed on the long stretches of trunk railroad routes throughout the USA.

A thoroughly workmanlike diesel-powered unit, this is an EMD GP-9 locomotive of the Rio Grande system pictured in 1972.

ducing the Pullman dining car so that passengers could eat better meals in greater comfort. A few years later, the same concept was adopted in Europe by a Belgian, Georges Nageimackers, as the Compagnie des Wagon-Lits.

Both Pullman and Wagon-Lits facilities were aimed at providing the first-class passenger with luxury. It was a British company, the Midland Railway, that first saw the advantages of appealing to the second- and third-class travelers, by offering greater comfort within the standard fare. In the short term, this improvement cost the com-

This Alco FPA-3 locomotive was photographed in 1962. While lacking the "flavor" of steam-powered locomotives. Such diesel-powered units are highly practical for modern railroad operators wanting reliability and economy in operations in which freight is now far more important in economic terms than passengers.

This EMD F-7A locomotive was photographed in 1988, and is thoroughly representative of the type of diesel-powered locomotive now used for all long-distance routes in the continental USA.

Short-distance railroad routes in the US are now limited almost exclusively to commuter services, linking major cities with their dormitory towns. This is such as service, with double-decker cars, pulled by a Fairbanks-Morse *Trainmaster* locomotive.

pany quite heavily, but in the longer term, it more than paid for itself by attracting a far higher volume of traffic. The company also appreciated the value of speed, and pioneered the notion of high-speed travel. The notion caught on at once in Britain and the USA, but was less popular on the more regulated railroads of mainland Europe.

Locomotion had achieved a speed of 15mph with a 48-ton load; by the end of the 19th century, express trains were regularly achieving 75mph or more, and even greater speeds were attained in the first quarter of the 20th century with the streamlining of locomotives and further improvement of their mechanical features. This development also allowed the building of huge engines able to haul very heavy loads over long distances, and enabled the movement of vast quantities of coal and mineral ores in countries such as Australia, Canada, South Africa, and the United States.

For its first 50 years, the steam locomotive had no real rival. There were, of course, a modest number of traction engines using steam for their motive power, but they were best employed for agricultural use as their heavy weight and low speed made them poorly suited for road transport. But, in 1879, at the Berlin Trades' Exhibition, Werner von Siemens demonstrated the world's first electric railroad. It was a mere 1,800ft long, but was clearly an omen of the road (or rather railroad track) ahead: in 1906, the world's first mainline electrification was completed in Switzerland, on the route to Italy via the Simplon tunnel, and electrification became increasingly common for commuter trains in the 1920s and 1930s.

Another competitor for the steam locomotive was the diesel locomotive, generally operating on the diesel-electric principle with the diesel powering an electric generator that supplies current to the drive motors. Whereas the steam locomotive requires massive quantities of coal and water, needs a halt for the removal of soot and ash at eight-hour intervals, and generates a mass of smoke, the diesel requires only modest amounts of diesel oil, does not need a cleaning

This poster extols the London and North Eastern Railways Coronation class service, using streamlined locomotives for the fast service linking London's Kings Cross station with Scottish destinations.

Photographed in 1988, but somehow redolent of an altogether earlier age, this is a 4-6-2 Pacific class locomotive crossing a river bridge.

halt, and generates far lower pollution levels. The diesel came into its own during the 1930s and was fully proven in World War II, resulting n a wholesale turn against steam locomotives in the 1940s: it is estimated that in the USA alone, some 40,000 steam locomotives were replaced by diesel locomotives and scrapped in the years between 1940 and 1960. This was in itself a period of great trial for the railroads, which were suffering catastrophic declines in passenger loads as the airlines began to attract their long-distance travelers, in the same way that the automobile had hit shorter-distance rail travel in the 1920s and 1930s.

In the Western world, the steam locomotive is now a rarity in all but its preserved form, but in many Third World countries where the cost of electrification or oil imports is high, the steam locomotive is still alive and running magnificently: many smaller countries operate elderly steam locomotives, but in countries such as China, and South Africa, the abundance of local coal supplies is reflected in continued production of awesomely large and efficient steam locomotives.

One of the classic railroad trips that remains intact in the mid-1990s, although not for much longer, is the Canadian Pacific Railroad's transcontinental service linking the Canadian east and west coasts. Note the observation cars that are one of the main attractions of this route through some of the finest scenery in the world.

One of the attractions of electricity over diesel fuel for locomotive power is its ecological friendliness in urban areas. It is also easier to install and maintain the overhead wires used to supply the electricity to the locomotive via a moving pantograph. This is such a locomotive of the Amtrak system, photographed in 1982.

Long-distance routes often demand the use of coupled locomotives when a heavy load has to be pulled, or where there is a steep gradient. This is such a train of the Amtrak system in the USA.

Cars

The first vehicles that could travel on a road without some form of external power, such as animals to pull them were steam-powered machines. In 1769, for example, the French pioneer Nicolas Cugnot, who was a captain in the French army, designed and built a three-wheeled steam tractor which he intended for the towing of artillery pieces. The vehicle made its first run in 1770, and its capabilities included a maximum speed of 3mph (5km/h) and the ability to move for between 10 and 15 minutes before a halt had to be called for the boiler to build up sufficient pressure of steam for continued movement. In design, the Cugnot tractor had an open flatbed chassis with two spoked wooden wheels at the back on a simple axle, and a single spoked wheel at the front. The single wheel was turned by a simple piston engine, supplied with steam from a large boiler hanging over the front of the vehicle, and could be steered by levers operated by the driver. The Cugnot tractor worked, but it was a far from practical vehicle because of its need for frequent stops, its retention of primitive wheels, and its total lack of any type of suspension.

Cugnot and a few other experimenters in the second half of the 18th century saw the steam-powered road vehicle as an alternative to draft animals for the movement of heavy loads. It was the beginning of the 19th century before the concept of the powered road vehicle for passenger transport began to achieve any currency. It was in 1801, for example, that Richard Trevithick, that great British pioneer of steam power and the primitive railroad, built a four-wheeled steam-powered wagon, and in the 1830s Sir Richard Gurney built a six-wheeled steam wagon. The Gurney machine reached a speed of 15mph (24km/h) in one trial, a prodigious effort that must have shaken the bones of all

The Roper Steam Carriage was one of the USA's first automobiles. It was built in 1865 by Sylvester H.Roper.

Right: Having been used already on a motorcycle and a river launch, the internal combustion engine designed by Daimler was installed in a four-wheeled road vehicle in 1886 and proved practical. The single-cylinder engine had a displacement of 469 cc and developed 1.5 hp at 700 rpm, and this allowed the Daimler vehicle to reach a speed of 10 mph.

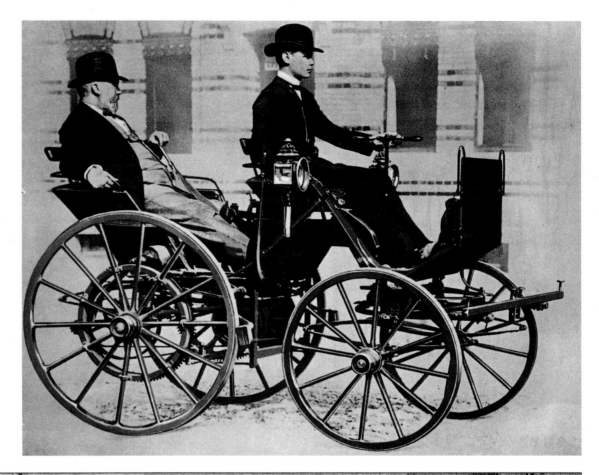

Below: The development of the British automobile was almost fatally slowed by legislation that up to 1896, demanded that any motor vehicle on the public road system had to be preceded by a man with a red flag (day) or red lantern (night).

Left: The Daimler automobile of 1886 had four seat accommodation, with two persons on the higher bench seat forward of the engine and two more persons on the lower seat to the rear of the engine. A belt drive was used to power the rear wheels, and the front wheels were steered by a vertical shaft with four handles.

Below left: Between 1900 and 1911, the White company of the USA produced a long series of steam-powered automobiles, before switching to gasoline-powered engines in belated recognition of the fact that the steam engine could not offer long-term competition to the internal combustion engine.

on board, for the roads of the time were hard on vehicles without adequate suspension. The Gurney steam wagon was just one of several such types, and by the middle of the 1830s there were a number of passenger services being operated by such steam wagons, some of which could carry as many as 22 persons.

That progress was made, and continued to be made, was something of a tribute to the perseverance of their designers and operators, for these steam wagons were generally not popular. The wagons were very noisy and cumbersome, their presence frightened the horses that were currently the most popular form of transport, they generated masses of black coal smoke, and their cinders were a liability to urban

Above: In its definitive form, the White steam engine was a compound two-cylinder unit of the double effect type developing some 20 hp. Like all steam engines, it took a comparatively long time to develop power, and then required frequent replenishment of the water supply.

Right: The 20-hp Darracq was one of the first genuinely successful French automobiles, and was one of the machines that set the pace of development in the formative years between the closing stages of the 19th century and the beginning of the 20th century.

Below right: The Ford Quadricycle of 1896 was a primitive vehicle, but the encouragement of Thomas Alva Edison persuaded Henry Ford to persevere, and become one of the decisive figures in the history of the automobile.

Below: The Daimler of 1894 was typical of the type of early automobile that drew its inspiration from the horse-drawn buggy. This tendency was emphasized by items such as the fringed cover.

and country life alike. Cinders from steam wagons were blamed for the destruction of several wooden bridges and the frequent incineration of field crops.

Gradually the steam wagon improved in capability and began to secure a measure of public acceptance. As the type's numbers and capabilities grew, however, there was increasing pressure against them from the operators of coach lines and – in a neat reversal of history, by an industry that had itself not long ago been castigated as a public menace – by railroad operators. As the result of pressure from opponents to the steam wagon, therefore, the 1865 Locomotives Act limited steam wagons to a speed of 4mph and 2mph (6.4km/h and

Car racing

The invention of motor racing, and its organization as a major sport, must both be credited to the French. This was largely because the British were restricted in speed until the passing in 1896, of the Light Automotive Act, that raised the open-road speed limited to 20 mph. By this time France had already witnessed several races.

The first of these was possibly the steam tricycle race of April 1887 in Paris, which attracted only one entrant but drew three competitors in 1891, but the first properly constituted event was the Paris-Rouen race of July 1894. The 1894 race drew many entrants that were whittled down to 21 (14 gasoline- and seven steam-powered vehicles) in a series of qualifying heats. The race was decided not only in terms of speed but also of manageability, safety, and economy. Thus Bouton was first over the line in his De Dion-Bouton, but shared first prize with Peugeot and Panhard-Levassor who both used the reliable and fuel economical Daimler engine built under licence by Panhard-Levassor. The first officially recognized race was another city-to-city event, in this instance the Paris-Bordeaux race of June 1895. There followed a series of 23 such races run by the Automobile Club de France.

These races included the first international event to and from Paris via Amsterdam in 1898 and the great Paris-Madrid race that ended the series in May 1903. This last race attracted 179 starters, many of them in huge vehicles with engines of up to 20-liter capacity for speeds of up to 75 mph, but there were so many casualties (including five drivers and mechanics as well as numbers of the estimated 3 million spectators along the route) that the French authorities ordered the race to be abandoned at

Bordeaux. It was only in 1927 that this type of long-distance road race was resumed with the inauguration of the Mille Miglia in Italy and the Transamerican in the USA.

Road races were replaced in the short term by long-distance rallies and circuit races. The first great rally was the 1907 event between Peking and Paris via Siberia. This attracted five entrants, and it took the winner two months to cover the distance. The winner was Prince Scipione Borghese in his 40-hp Itala driven by Ettore Guizzardi with Luigi Barsini, a journalist, as passenger.

Soon similar races were inaugurated in several other countries, and arrangements were also made in many regions for roads to be closed to the public for short times so that speed trials could be run. The first purpose-designed racing circuit was opened in July 1907 at Brooklands in the UK. Racing circuits were soon developed on other countries, and thus began the type of motor racing that is still the most popular aspect of the sport. Notable American circuits of the period were William K. Vanderbiltís Long Island Motor Parkway of 1908, and the Indianapolis Speedway of 1909, where the first Indianapolis 500 race was run two years later.

Clockwise from the top right, the vehicles pictured on this spread are the 1903 Dietrich in the Paris-Madrid race, the Renault in the same race, the 1914 Mercedes, and the 1914 Fiat.

Left: Another vehicle clearly little more than a motorized version of a current horse-drawn type was this electric automobile owned by Queen Alexandra, wife of King Edward VII.

Below left: This humble workshop was the birthplace of the Ford Model T, perhaps the most important automobile that the world had ever seen.

3.2km/h) on country roads and urban roads respectively, and demanded that all such vehicles be preceded by a man on foot to warn of the steam vehicle's approach: this man had to carry and wave a red flag by day and a red lantern by night. It was 1876 before the provisions of the Locomotives Act were eased in any respect, and 1896 before the Act was finally repealed. (There is little doubt, however, that the effect of the Act was to delay the development of the automobile in the UK for some 30 years.)

The development of steam wagons was not, of course, a British prerogative. In the USA for example, the first real pioneer in this field was Oliver Evans, an inventor and enthusiast of the capabilities of the steam engine. In 1805, Evans made an extraordinary steam-powered dredger for the deepening of the harbor of Philadelphia, Pennsylvania. This

machine weighted some 32,000lb, and comprised a steam wagon that could also operate as a flatboat. The Evans vehicle is the first known example of a vehicle that could move under its own power on land and in the water.

Other steam vehicles were developed in the USA during the 19th century, the development of such American vehicles paralleling that of similar vehicles in Europe. Toward the end of the century, however, there was a spate of vehicles designed by men such as J N Carhart, Richard Dudgeon and Sylvester H Roper. In 1865, Roper built a trim four-wheeled steam cart that was clearly derived conceptually from the buggies of the period, with the driver seated high above the flatbed chassis and the steam powerplant installed behind the axle for the rear wheels, which were driven by the engine.

Such was the relatively high level of

Top: The company that stayed loyal to the steam car longer than any other was that of the Stanley twins, who tested their first such vehicle in 1887, and used steam engines right up to 1929, achieving considerable performance and reliability in the process.

Above: This Wolseley two-seater automobile of 1904 was typical of its period in the UK with comfortable upholstered but open accommodation. The engine was a 6-hp unit.

The Rover 20-hp tourer of 1907 was a British automobile offering moderately good performance and considerable comfort.

The Austin Grand Prix racing automobile of 1908 was fitted with a 100-hp engine, and achieved very respectable straight-line performance, although its road-holding and cornering, in common with those of all other contemporary vehicles, was lamentable by the standards of even a short time later.

The Austin 30-hp Tourer of 1907 epitomizes the era of the "sit up and beg" type of automobile in which virtually every line appears to be vertical or horizontal.

The Albion A6 Tourer of 1906-14 was a British automobile with its rear wheels powered by a chain drive from a 4,140-cc engine rated at 24 hp at 1,200 rpm. The top speed was 40 mph, and the type was a very successful automobile in the luxury class.

The Rover Landaulette of 1912 was a British automobile with a 2,200-cc four-cylinder engine rated at 12 hp, and was successfully aimed at the "quality" market.

Another automobile aimed at the British quality market was the Austin Town Carriage of 1911, with a 15-hp engine and, as with the Rover Landaulette, the chauffeur was separated from the passenger compartment by a glass screen.

success secured by steam-powered vehicles on American roads that it was such a machine that secured the world's first export order. This was for a vehicle designed by Ransom Eli Olds, and this was shipped to Bombay in 1893.

More than a hundred American companies built steam automobiles, and the most famous of them were the companies of Abner Doble and of the twin brothers Francis E and Freelan O Stanley. The Stanley company was in existence between 1897 and 1942, and produced a number of classic steam-powered automobiles that achieved very creditable performance, including, in the hands of Glenn Curtiss, later a celebrated aircraft pioneer, a world speed record in excess of 100 mph (161 km/h).

Despite this type of performance, the steam-powered automobile could never have become the dominant form of road transport, for the type took too long to raise a head of steam before any movement could be undertaken, had to stop frequently for fresh water and fuel, and inspired in many possible customers considerable dread of its large and very hot boiler and open fire .

An alternative that became viable in the late 19th century was the electric car, which had the advantages of being virtually silent, quick to start, and easy to operate. The first such automobiles appeared in

Opposite: The Commer Commercial was an early type of British bus, and helped pave the way for the use of motor vehicles for public transport.

In September 1914, the tide of World War I was turned in the 1st Battle of the Marne when extra Allied troops were rushed to the battle in Parisian taxicabs, such as the one illustrated, and buses, thereby halting the German advance.

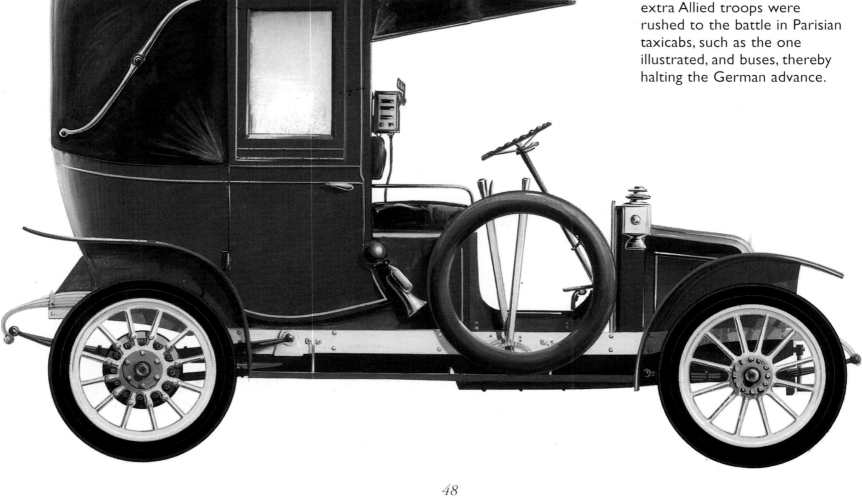

American use during the 1890s, and the most successful of the electric automobile builders was William Morrison of Des Moines, Iowa, which produced his first machine in 1890. Although it offered many advantages over the steam-powered automobile, the electrically powered automobile had two fairly distinct disadvantages: the maximum speed was generally less than 20mph (32km/h), and even at a considerably lower speed, the batteries were exhausted after a distance of some 50 miles (80km).

Even as the electrically powered automobile was enjoying its brief moment in the sunshine of public success, its eventual successor was already under development with an engine powered by gasoline or, as it is known to the British, petrol. The origins of this type of automobile, which is characterized by the use of an internal-combustion engine, can be traced back to the late 1850s. At this time a French pioneer, Etienne Lenoir, designed and built a single-cylinder internal-combustion engine, using as its fuel the same type of gas that was currently used for street and house lighting. In 1863, Lenoir installed his engine in

The Austin 7 "Chummy" tourer of 1922 was an early and successful attempt to make the automobile available to less affluent members of British society. Some 300,000 of the type were built with a 696-cc (later 747-cc) four-cylinder engine.

AS SILENT AS ITS SHADOW

Rolls Royce

At a meeting in May 1904 the Hon. Charles Rolls and Henry Royce, respectively the British importer of Panhard automobiles from France and a producer of electrical cranes and dynamos, decided to join forces for the creation of very high quality automobiles. Rolls supplied cachet and a clientele, while Royce provided the engineering capability within the basic concept of "take and existing part and make it better." This policy has been followed ever since, and has meant that Rolls-Royce automobiles are not innovative, but rather the ultimate expression in quality and reliability of existing engineering practices. The early Rolls-Royce automobiles gained a reputation for comfort and luxury that are still the hallmarks of this classic marque. By the middle of the 1990s Rolls-Royce had produced about 100,000 automobiles, and perhaps 60% of these vehicles still exist – there can hardly be a better testimony to the type.

The first classic from Rolls-Royce was the *Silver Ghost* that appeared in 1906 with the distinctive Doric arch at the top of its radiator that was supplemented in 1911 by the "Spirit of Ecstasy" emblem to create a front profile that have been hallmarks of the series ever since.

Rolls was killed in a flying accident in 1910, but Royce continued his search for automotive excellence. Two of the keys to the success and longevity of Rolls-Royce automobiles have always been the use only of first-class materials and the implementation of the strictest possible quality control criteria. One of the most innovative features of the early automobiles was a pressurized lubrication system, and the quality of the engines is attested by the fact that even in early machines the engine was good for some 20,000 miles without servicing. An electric starter motor was introduced only in 1919.

The *Silver Ghost* remained in production up to 1925 (and was used as the basis of an armored car in World War I), and was then replaced in the period up to World War II by the *Phantom*, the lower-cost *Twenty* and the *Silver Wraith*. Improved Silver Phantoms and Silver Wraiths were reintroduced after the war, and were later replaced by the *Silver Cloud*, *Silver Shadow*, *Silver Spirit* and *Silver Spur*.

Right: The ultimate expression in grand touring luxury is represented by the Rolls-Royce Corniche, which is the coupe version of the Silver Shadow introduced in 1971 with a General Motor Turbo-Hydromatic automatic transmission, independent front- and rear-wheel suspensions, and dual-circuit disc brakes on all four wheels.

In an effort to promote his Model B automobile, Henry Ford turning to racing. After announcing the fact that he would break the world land speed record, Ford proceeded to do so in January 1904, when he recorded a speed of 97.4 mph over the measured mile on a cinder-covered track created on the frozen surface of Lake St. Clair.

a very clumsy wheeled chassis, and this primitive internal-combustion vehicle managed to cover a distance of about 6 miles (10 km) in a time of two hours. The trouble with gas as the fuel for an internal-combustion engine is its low density, which means that in the absence of an effective system for compressing the gas and then storing it safely, the amount of fuel that could be carried was sufficient for only a very short trip. The answer lay with a fuel of higher density, and this was gasoline.

The honor of developing a successful gasoline-powered engine was shared by two German pioneers, who were working entirely independently of each other. In 1895 each man successfully completed the prototype of his gasoline-powered engine: Gottlieb Daimler installed

The first automobile built by Chevrolet's plant at Detroit, Michigan, in 1912 was this Classic Six. This was a high-priced vehicle aimed at the upper end of the market, and was powered by a 4,900-cc six-cylinder engine made separately in Flint, Ohio, by the Mason Motor Company, another enterprise within WC Durrant's General Motors empire.

A marque that disappeared as General Motors decided to concentrate on its Chrysler models was Chalmers. One of the last Chalmers models was this 1923 sedan that was typical of a type that had changed little since the middle of the previous decade in all but the adoption of a four-wheel hydraulic braking system.

his powerplant in a two-wheeled motorcycle, and Otto Benz fitted his engine in a three-wheeled carriage.

These were both very primitive machines, and the Benz automobile was little more advanced in all respects. Further developments were made in Germany and other European countries, but the evolution of the automobile toward its current form was largely due to French engineers. The two most important of these were Emile Levassor and René Panhard, who were partners in a coach-building concern. The two men built their first automobile, in 1890 powered by a Daimler engine, and in the following year Levassor introduced the front-mounted engine whose power was transmitted to the rear wheels, as in all other such vehicles, by a chain drive. In 1898, however, Louis

The Cadillac V16 of 1931 was the world's first production automobile with a V-16 engine, and was also one of the last with such an engine. The engine had a displacement of 7,390 cc and delivered 165 hp, and was noted for its power and smoothness. Later V-12 engines proved to be nearly as powerful and just as smooth without the V-16's added complexity and high fuel consumption.

The Plymouth PA Four of 1931 was a business coupe, and proved remarkably successful in terms of its sales as a time when many other American automobile manufacturers were forced to go out of business. The vehicle was powered by a four-cylinder engine with a capacity of 3,210 cc and delivering 56 hp to the rear wheels by means of a three-speed manual transmission. The automobile was decidedly stylish for its period, and was also offered in two- and four-door sedan forms, and in variants that included a roadster with a dickey seat, a convertible and a Phaeton.

The 1935 DeSoto Series SF Airstream sedan had a spacious interior, and this was one of the features that made the type attractive to operators such as taxi companies.

Below: Just before the US government stopped the production of automobiles for the duration of World War II, Ford's product line included the DeLuxe series as its mid-price range. Seen here is the Super DeLuxe station wagon, which retailed for $1,125.

Renault took the evolution of the automobile a step farther by the replacement of the chain drive by a shaft drive.

During the 1890s, the notion of the gasoline-powered automobile caught the attention of many American inventors, and it was in 1893-94 that the first such machine of American design was built by Charles E and J Frank Duryea. The vehicle suffered a breakdown on its first run in 1893, but was soon developed to a more reliable state, and made its first successful run in January 1894 in the town of Springfield, Massachusetts. In 1895, it is worth noting, the Duryea brothers established the first American automobile manufacturing company.

The Model T Phaeton was Ford's attempt to revive the commercial success of its product line with an updated version of a well proved basic design whose use of established components offered reliability as well as low cost.

Virtually a lower-cost version of the Chrysler Royal Six, the DeSoto was an attractive purchase for many middle-class Americans in the second half of the 1930s. The type was also adopted by several police forces as the large trunk of this coupe model provided ample volume for the bulky thermionic valve radio sets of the period.

Other American inventors involved with the development of the gasoline-powered automobile at this time were John W Lambert of Ohio City, and W T Harris of Louisville, Kentucky. At a slightly later date, other pioneers of the automobile industry were Henry Ford, Charles Brady King, Ransom Eli Olds and Alexander Winton.

The automobiles of this period were generally too expensive, in terms of purchase and operating costs, for most people. Two developments of 1901 started to change these factors. The cost of purchase was lowered by the introduction of mass production techniques, initially by Olds, and the cost of operating an automobile began to tumble as the first of many large oilfields was discovered in eastern

The 1937 Ford pick-up truck, seen here in de luxe form with bright trim on the windshield surround, grille bars and running boards, also witnessed the introduction of styling changes such as a two-piece windshield and also had a slightly longer freight box. Vehicles such as this were financially important to the manufacturing company and the persons of organizations that bought them. They were also of considerable impact at the social level, as evidence of the increasing reliance placed on gasoline-powered machines to undertake the tasks that had still seen the employment of horse-drawn vehicles in the second half of the 1920s.

The Ford DeLuxe Fordor sedan of 1938 introduced a remodelled front with a new grille and more acutely sloped hood. The cost of this model was $770, and the type is typical of the enclosed sedan that increasingly replaced the open-topped automobile as the typical family automobile during the course of the 1930s.

Sold to the extent of 429,000 vehicles in 1947, this Ford Super DeLuxe Sportsman convertible was little more than a reworking of the 1942 model, with wooden side and real panels. This four-seat two-door type was powered by a 3,925-cc V-8 engine delivering 100 hp, and secured much of its sales success from its break with the austerity concept prevalent during World War II.

The rapid switch from World War II-type austerity to the opulence and indeed ostentation of the 1950s is epitomized here by the 1950 Buick Model 79 Roadmaster station wagon with its size and large quantity of chrome and exterior wood. This four-door monster of the road turned the scales at 4,470 lb, and was driven by a 5,245-cc straight-eight engine delivering 152 hp to the rear axle by means of a two-speed automatic transmission.

Texas. The introduction of mass production techniques came about in 1901 as a result of the destruction by fire of the Olds Motor Works in Detroit. In an effort to maintain the flow of finished automobiles, Olds arranged for standardized parts and assemblies to be made at local machine shops, and then delivered to his rebuilt factory for assembly into complete vehicles; during assembly, vehicles were wheeled from one man to another for the installation of the next required component. So successful was the system that Olds built 425 automobiles in 1901, 3,750 in 1902, and 5,000 in 1903.

Another development of the mass production concept was introduced in 1908 by Henry M Leland of the Cadillac Automobile Company. This development involved interchangeable parts, so that a standard component could be used for the assembly or repair of any

The Dodge Custom four-door sedan of 1946 was typical of Dodge's reputation for building reliable and comfortable automobiles that lacked any real element of "flashiness." Typical of the period are the fairly boxy accommodation, the heavy cross-hatch radiator grille and the whitewall tires. The vehicle was powered by a 3,775-cc straight-six engine of somewhat venerable basic design, driving the rear wheels by means of a three-speed automatic transmission.

MG Cars

Founded in Oxford in the U.K. during the mid-1920s as Morris Garage but later better known as MG, this was the sports car branch of Morris. The first product of the new organization appeared in 1924 as the MG 14/28 HP version of the Morris Cowley Bullnose automobile with a 1,548-cc engine and a personalized body, but this four-seater was larger than the type of automobile required for the British market for sporting cars and was soon replaced by the two-seat Morris Midget based on the chassis of the Morris Minor automobile together with its four-cylinder engine with a capacity of 847cc. This opened the way for a series of small MG sports cars that soon acquired an excellent reputation for sturdiness, reliability and lively rather than high performance.

From the early 1930s a number of new MG models appeared with four- or six-cylinder engines, and these proved as successful on the racing tracks as in the hands of private owners on British roads. In 1935 MG was integrated into the revised Nuffield Organization and ceased production of sports cars in favor of saloon automobiles that culminated in the Type WA of 1939 after the introduction of the MG Type T Midget. After World War II there was another change in policy, and sports cars were built alongside the saloon automobiles as the T series and YA Magnette series respectively. In 1955 there appeared the MGA, of which 100,000 were sold, followed in 1962 by the classic MGB that was built in substantially larger numbers for the domestic and export markets in roadster and coupe forms.

The MG name disappeared after the 1968 merger that created the British Leyland Motor Company, and it was only in 1982 that it reappeared for a 'sporty' version of the British Leyland Metro small saloon automobile. There is now a small but thriving industry catering for the demand for preserved and rebuilt MG sports cars, which have become collectors items.

Above: The design philosophy that was to make MG cars attractive to large numbers of people wanting a sporty automobile, but lacking in the financial resources to purchase a genuine sports car such as a Bentley, is evident in "Old Number One" of 1925.

Opposite top: The MG Midget series culminated in the Type TF that was built into the mid-1950s with the same 1,300-cc engine used in the original Type TA of 1936. That same engine was used in the vehicle illustrated here, the MGA, but was uprated in this application to 69 hp and installed in a body of considerably more refined aerodynamic shape on an updated chassis.

Opposite bottom: In 1962, the MGA was replaced by the MGB, which is seen here in the form of the definitive MGB GT that appeared in 1980 with a new radiator grille and bumper together with a 1,800-cc engine.

example of any given model of automobile. The success of the concept was proved after Cadillac shipped three automobiles to the UK, where they were disassembled and their components jumbled together before mechanics then reassembled the vehicles without problem.

This trend toward mass production was taken to its ultimate point by Henry Ford, who saw in the concept the ideal means of making the automobile affordable to the mass of the American people. The effect of Ford's introduction of the moving assembly line was a decrease in the cost of the Model T from $850 in 1908 to $400 in 1916. This was one of the primary reasons for the Model T production total of 15 million between 1908 and 1927, and also explains why half of the automobiles sold in the USA during this time were Ford machines. In the second half of the 1920s, however, Ford was overtaken as the USA's largest manufacturer of automobiles by General Motors, which had been established in 1908 by William C Durant to combine Buick, Cadillac, Oakland, Oldsmobile and seven other automobile manufacturers.

As noted in the section below dealing with military transport, the automobile became increasingly important during World War I. The

Below: One of the greatest of all sports cars was the Mercedes 540-K built between 1934 and 1939. The vehicle was powered by a 5,400-cc eight-cylinder engine delivering 115 hp or, with the aid of a supercharger, 180 hp. Other features were hydraulic brakes and independent all-round suspension.

demands of the war placed greater emphasis on reliability and payload capacity and, by requiring large numbers of standardized vehicles at modest cost, further emphasized the need for truly effective mass production techniques. The USA became the main supplier of automobiles and their related heavier transport kin in World War I, and in the aftermath of the war the automobile completely superseded other means of transport in the countries of the civilized world. The importance of the automobile is attested by the fact that in 1919, the auto industry was third in the value of its products in the American market, being exceeded only by the meat packing and iron/steel industries.

During the 1920s, the production of automobiles in the USA and Canada increased dramatically as mass production lowered the price of the vehicles, the social and political climates were right for this development, and at a time of relatively full employment and a booming economy, people had money in their pockets. Automobile sales rose from 1.905 million in 1920 to 4.455 million in 1929, the year in which the 'Great Depression' began and the automobile industry went into a decline together with virtually every other element of the North American manufacturing industrial base. As the sales of automobiles boomed during the 1920s, the number of manufacturers declined from 108 in 1923 to 44 in 1927, as the larger manufacturers consolidated the advantages by mass production to force their smaller competitors into mergers or liquidation. The three companies that profited most strongly from this tendency were General Motors, Ford and Chrysler, which emerged as the true giants of world automobile production.

The market leader in the early 1920s was Ford, and in 1921 more than half of the automobiles sold in the USA were of Ford manufacture.

Above: Based in Dearborn, Michigan, Ford was naturally enough the supplier of the city's fire and ambulance forces. The ambulance seen here is a specially equipped version of the 1952 Courier, and the fire engines are of a model based on the F-750 truck chassis with special bodywork and equipment.

Unable to compete with Ford in terms of low price, the other manufacturers decided to offer automobiles with greater comfort and more advanced automotive features. This established the trend toward a line of new or at least upgraded models each year, at a time when Ford was content to concentrate on the mass production of the Model T. The other manufacturers had cleverly appreciated the tenor of the times, which demanded change, and therefore appreciated the yearly advent of new models. The company that first profited from this trend was Chevrolet, one of the General Motors marques, which overtook Ford in sales during 1927 and thereby precipitated the end of Model T production, as Ford finally appreciated the need to update its product line.

The 1920s were also marked by a radical change in the shape and nature of the automobile. Up to this time, the automobile had been in essence the horse-drawn buggy, revised for propulsion by an inter-

On altogether smaller scale, this diminutive British fire engine was a 1952 model based on the Morris Minor saloon.

Top: Powered by a 1,490-cc four-cylinder engine delivering 60 hp, the MG Magnette was the first of this manufacturerís automobiles to have a unitary body shell.

Below right: The Austin Healey 3000 Mk II of 1959 was a classic British sports car with a 2,910-cc six-cylinder engine delivering 130 hp.

nal-combustion engine, and therefore of very 'boxy' appearance with an open body that could be covered by a fabric hood erected on frames. From the period after World War I, however, the enclosed body became increasingly the norm: in 1919, 90per cent of all automobiles were of the open type, but 10 years later this situation had been reversed, and 90 per cent of all automobiles were of the enclosed type. The vehicle regarded as the precurser of this trend was the Essex of 1922.

Other changes introduced in the 1920s were quieter and more powerful engines that were also considerably more reliable, electric starter motors to obviate the need for a hand-cranked start, four- rather than two-wheel braking, quick-drying cellulose paints for a smoother and more durable finish, sealed-beam lights, shatterproof glass, independent suspension systems, wider tires that worked effectively at lower pressures, and factory-installed 'luxuries' such as heaters and radios.

This trend continued in the 1930s. In 1932, Ford introduced the first low-priced automobile with a V-8 engine for improved performance and smoother running, De Soto pioneered a streamlined styling concept with the Airflow in 1934, the 1935 Pontiac introduced an all-steel top, and by 1939 the pace of technical development had reached the point that General Motors was able to offer an automatic transmission system on the medium-priced Oldsmobile.

Above right: The Austin A 90 Atlantic convertible of 1948 was a British two-door automobile that did not achieve sales success.

Right: The Rover P4 was one of a series of luxury cars from this British manufacturer in the 1940s and 1950s, this being a P4 75 of 1951.

Top: The Ford Customline four-door sedan of 1953 was marketed as an automobile for "middle America," and as such was a no-fuss machine offering reliability and comfort at an affordable price.

Below: Available with a detachable hard top, the 1957 Ford Thunderbird was typical of the automobile extravagance of this period. It was a two-seater weighing 3,145 lb with a V-8 engine of 4,875-cc capacity delivering 212 hp to the rear wheels by means of a three-speed automatic transmission.

Like all other elements of Western manufacturing industry, the automobile industry suffered from the effects of the financial Depression that followed the 'Crash' of 1929. In 1931, the American automobile industry delivered its 50-millionth vehicle, but sales in that year were also 2.5 million less than in 1929, and in 1932 sales fell to 1.14 million. The effect on the automobile industry was to hasten the demise of many small manufacturers: in 1930, General Motors, Ford and Chrysler already had 80 per cent of the US automobile market, and by 1939 this figure had increased to 90 per cent.

Yet despite these problems, the automobile continued to increase its hold on the public consciousness of the USA and, to a lesser extent, other Western countries. Sales of automobiles in the USA averaged 3.2 million per year between 1935 and 1941, and the demand for better transportation was reflected in the growth of surfaced roads, whose total mileage increased from almost 0.4 million miles (0.6 million km) in 1921, to 1.3 million miles (2.2 million km) in 1940.

It was at this stage that World War II intervened, and the USA soon became the 'arsenal of democracy' for the supply of weapons not only to its own forces but also to those of the other Allied powers fighting Germany, Italy and Japan. Even though the United States did not

Right: The Cadillac Coupe de Ville of 1959 was a two-seat coupe weighing 4,720 lb and powered by a 6,390-cc Ve-8 engine delivering 325 hp to the rear wheels. In an apt description, one critic had said that the fins "would have made Buck Rogers blush."

Opposite center: The 1953 Chevrolet Corvette was the USA's first sports car, and included among its features a fiberglass body. The type met initial customer resistance (only 315 were built in the first year), but went on to become a classic. The engine was a somewhat obsolescent six-cylinder unit delivering 150 hp, and the car's weight was 2,705 lb. The Corvette went on to become the USA's most enduring sports car in a number of models that have all become legendary.

Below: This Ford Skyliner is seen in the turquoise and white color scheme that was very popular in 1959, the year in which this model was taken off the market to leave the Sunliner as Ford's only convertible.

enter the war until December 1941, production of civil transport had already been reduced so that industry could supply mainly British and French orders for trucks and other military transport. Sales of automobiles in the USA fell to just 223,000 in 1942 and then virtually stopped, as the American automobile industry turned to the production and delivery of more than 2.6 million trucks, 600,000 Jeeps and more than 49,000 tanks, as well as 10 per cent of aircraft, 75 per cent of aero engines, 47 per cent of machine guns and 87 per cent of air-dropped bombs.

After World War II, most of this industrial capacity was available for a resumption of the automobile industry. Deprived of new vehicles during the war years, and with many more people now accustomed to the concept of travel within the country even if not overseas, the American public once again took to the automobile, which emerged

Top: In 1965 Ford introduced the Thunderbird Limited Edition Special Landau, of which a mere 4,500 were built. It had a $50 package of extras that included "Ember-Glo" metallic paint with matching wheel covers, parchment vinyl top, a wood-like interior trim and even a plaque inscribed with the owneris name!

Center: Combining high customer appeal and genuine off-road capability, the Range Rover is a comfortable but practical vehicle based on a 3,500-cc V-8 engine licensed from General Motors and built in aluminum. From the early 1980s the type has also been offered in a diesel-engined form with a licensed Italian VM engine.

Below: The only American production-line convertible of its period, the Cadillac Eldorado Convertible was a 5,100-lb machine powered by a V-8 engine of 8,200-cc capacity. The $12,000 price tag included automatic transmission, air conditioning, FM/AM radio, and steel-belted radial tires.

Top: This Chevrolet Corvette was the 1978 version, and retained the same type of fiberglass body albeit in a much sleeker form looking far more aggressive than the 1953 original.

Above right: The Pontiac Grand Prix was introduced in 1972, a year in which it was sold to the extent of 93,000 examples. It was produced only as a two-door hardtop with a 6,600-cc V-8 engine driving an automatic transmission.

Center: With front-wheel drive and a transversely mounted 848-cc engine, the Austin Mini was introduced in 1959 as a cheap and very maneuverable little automobile. The type is still in production during 1995 with the larger 998-cc engine introduced in 1984.

Right: The most popular Ford since World War II and the most successful American sports car of all time, the Ford Mustang was introduced in 1964 and sold over 500,000 examples up to the end of 1965. In 1967 the type was revised with the bodywork illustrated here. The 2+2 version sold for $2,590.

Exotic Cars

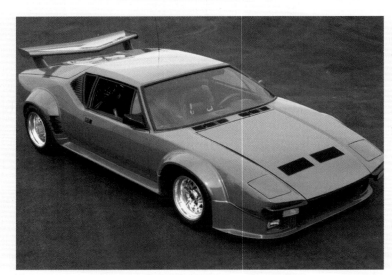

Between the two world wars, the three countries that dominated the world market as coachbuilders were France, the UK and the USA, and each evolved along lines that reflected the national characteristics of these three countries. After World War II, the country that emerged as the giant of the coach-building world was Italy, which has now held this position for some 50 years and in the process altered the world's perception of what is beautiful in the design of cars.

The main trend in this process has been the replacement of extremely curvaceous and sumptuous lines by no less esthetic lines dictated by the desire to incorporate the latest materials in a blend of subtler angles and curves that combine advanced

aerodynamic and structural thinking for minimized drag, and reduced weight consonant with the strength required for durability and, in a process that has become increasingly important in recent years, the protection of passengers in the event of an accident.

The first of the great Italian designers was Battista 'Pinin' Farina, who died in 1966 after contributing in large measure to the success of several Ferrari, Peugeot, Alfa Romeo and Austin designs, and was followed by his son Sergio and son-in-law Renzo Carli. In 1975, Pininfarina became the first foreign designer of a Rolls-Royce automobile, the *Camargue*.

Giovanni Bertone and his son Giuseppe were notable for their practical work with Lancia, Lamborghini, Fiat, Volkswagen and Citroen, and also for their futuristic stylings such as the Chevrolet Testudo of

1963 and Chevrolet Ramarro of 1984.

Founded in 1968 by Giorgio Giugiaro, Ital Design had produced a number of classic designs for Alfa Romeo, BMW, Volkswagen, Lancia and Seat in Europe, Hyundai in South Korea and Isuzu in Japan.

Owned by Ford since 1975, Ghia began in 1915, and rose to prominence in the period after 1945, when it received commissions for a number of 'dream automobile' designs from Chrysler, Ford and Packard. The company also designed a number of production automobiles including types for Renault, Volvo and Volkswagen, as well as classic sports cars such as the De Tomaso Mangusta and Pantera. Ghia was also responsible for the Probe III design on which the well-known Ford Sierra was based.

Other notable Italian coachbuilders include Zagato that was established in 1929 and in more recent years designed the Aston Martin DB4 and Alfa Romeo TZ,;Giovanni Michelotti who was responsible for the BMWs of the 1960s, the Isuzu Skyline Sport and two British types, the Triumph Herald and Triumph TR5, Touring that was responsible for several Alfa Romeo, Ferrari, Lancia, Lamborghini and BMW designs; and Alfredo Vignale who was responsible for a number of customized bodies on Ferrari, Rolls-Royce, Cadillac, BMW and Mercedes chassis.

The influence of these and other Italian designers is readily discernible in the exotic automobiles pictured on this spread, and it would be hard to over-emphasize the importance of Italian design concepts in the creation of the modern automobile.

from the war in a more flamboyant form, and with considerably more powerful engines in longer, lower and wider vehicles.

It was not just these obvious features that changed, for the automobiles of the later 1940s and early 1950s also featured larger curved windshields, larger rear windows, tinted glass, automatic transmission in many mid-priced vehicles, and the use of engine power for power steering, air conditioning, the braking system and even for the operation of convertible automobiles' opening and closing roofs.

Throughout this period the USA produced more automobiles than all other countries combined, and up to the end of the 1970s, still produced one-quarter of the world output. During most of this period, the

Below left: Introduced in 1961 as one of the most impressive of all British sports cars, the Jaguar E Type was offered in coupe and roadster versions. In its original form the E-Type had a six-cylinder engine of 3,780-cc capacity delivering 269 hp, but in 1964 the engine capacity was increased to 4,200 cc.

Below: The Chevrolet Corvette remains the ultimate expression of the purely American sports car. Although it perhaps something of an oversimplification, this can be construed as meaning the application of brute power where European designers would opt for greater finesse.

Right: The American sports car philosophy is probably stronger nowhere than in the love of the 'super stock' concept, in which a standard car is heavily modified internally without much external change. This is a Chevrolet Corvette, generally known just as the "Vette."

Above: Dragsters have very high-powered engines generally running on exotic fuels and installed as close as possible to the large rear wheels with their wide tires. The chassis is as light as possible, especially at its front end, and a braking 'chute is usually fitted for rapid deceleration at the end of the timed run.

rest of the world generally took its technical and commercial lead from the USA but this situation began to alter in the 1960s as the automobile industries of Western Europe and then Japan started to accelerate. Non-American automobiles were usually smaller than their American counterparts as they had to be used on generally more congested roads, and the higher price of fuel outside the USA placed a premium on smaller engines. These tendencies were reflected by American automobile production during the 1980s, but by that time, much of the world market had been captured by Japanese and local industries, and foreign imports (especially of Japanese automobiles) began to make an ever-increasing impact on American sales.

The world tendency in automobiles is now firmly committed to smaller and more economical cars that are safer to drive and have a reduced impact, in both manufacture and use, on an environment increasingly threatened by road-building, automobiles, and the larger forms of overland transport.

Motorcycles

The motorcycle was a logical development of the pedal cycle making use of the newly invented internal-combustion engine to replace leg power as the motive force. The earliest motorcycles were in fact motorized tricycles, and such vehicles were pioneered during the later 1880s in Germany by Gottlieb Daimler and in the UK by Edward Butler. After 1896 several types of motor tricycle, of which the most successful was the Ariel of 1899, entered production in British factories, but it was 1900 before the first genuinely practical belt-driven motorcycle was built in Paris, by Werner. The lead in the development and production of these vehicles soon returned to the UK, where the Excelsior and Quadrant types entered production in 1902. The main problems of motorcycles in this period were poor reliability, difficulties with the belt drive, and the lack of gears, but as these limitations were overcome the motorcycle emerged as an attractive and reliable form of transport. By the outbreak of World War I in 1914 there were several types with a combined belt and chain drives together with a gearbox. World War I saw rapid development of the motorcycle as the ideal machine for dispatch riders, and the companies that emerged from that war as the world leaders in motorcycle design were Douglas and Triumph.

Between the two world wars the British capitalized on this technical lead with the Germans and Italians as their main rivals, but led the world in the manufacture of all

types of motorcycle for the export as well as domestic markets. This period witnessed the advent of Norton as one of the main manufacturers of high-powered motorcycles. The attractiveness of British motorcycles on the world market was enhanced by a string of major racing successes throughout the 1920s and 1930s. During World War II, motorcycles were widely employed by the armies of both sides for the delivery of messages and also for reconnaissance.

The period after World War II was again dominated in its early period by British motorcycles except in the USA, where there was still a strong attachment to larger and higher-powered motorcycles of the type produced by companies such as Harley Davidson. As they started to rebuild their war-shattered economies, German and Italian manufacturers concentrated instead on the considerably lower-powered scooter with smaller wheels and improved weather protection. Gradually these companies returned to the motorcycle arena with machines that first rivaled and then exceeded the more traditional British motorcycles in both technical sophistication and performance.

This trend was also evident in Japan, where an emerging motorcycle manufacturing industry concentrated first on simple models that could be produced in large numbers very cheaply, and then on machines of increasing sophistication. Racing success had meanwhile switched from the British to the Germans and Italians, but these two countries were then eclipsed in terms of proved performance by the flood of Japanese motorcycles that

now dominate the world market although there remain niches for specialist machines of American, German and Italian manufacture.

Far left: This is a Zenith motorcycle, typical of the type pioneered by the British in the period between the world wars.

Top: Motorcycle racing is a highly popular sport.

Above: This is the engine of a Harley Davidson motorcycle, conservative in design but well proved and much loved by the marque's afficionados.

Military Vehicles

Throughout history, the armies of the world have needed some form of transport: vehicles for the movement of men and equipment rather than for fighting. From earliest times to the beginning of the 20th century, armies tried to live off the land in which they were operating, but still needed transport vehicles for the movement of heavy equipment, additional food supplies, ammunition and, in all too many cases, the officers' baggage and furniture. Hand carts provided a measure of transport capability, but more effective by far were animal-drawn wagons: oxen, though slow, were used for the heavy equipment, while horses and mules provided greater speed, but lower power. Generals encouraged their animals, like their men, to live off the land, but this was seldom possible in a campaign lasting more than a few weeks, and the result was that much of the available transport had to be allocated to the movement of fodder. One positive side to the use of animal transport, however, was the possibility of using the animals for food if the supply situation became impossible.

Well-conducted armies tried to keep non-essential elements to a minimum to avoid overwhelming their limited transport services, but there are many examples of armies in which the men had to go short of food, medicine, ammunition, or other vital

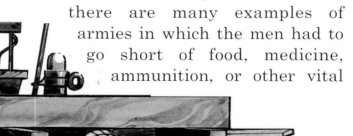

Even with the arrival of the powered truck as a major force in World War I, demand was still so much higher than supply that there was still need for very large quantities of animal-drawn transport, and also for derivatives of such transport to be towed as trailers behind powered vehicles.

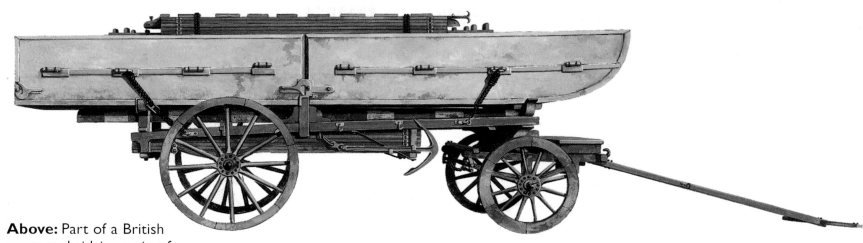

Above: Part of a British pontoon bridging train of World War I, each cart carrying one pontoon, its anchor or anchors plus chain and rope, and sufficient bridging material to tie the pontoon to its neighbors and provide the pedestrian footway or vehicle carriageway that would eventually complete the crossing of the water barrier being bridged.

Below: The British provided their heavy artillery with a measure, although only a small measure, of tactical mobility by the use of traction engines, which were heavy and slow but offered a capability unrivaled in contemporary vehicles for the towing of heavy loads under adverse conditions. This is a Daimler-Foster tractor with a 105-hp Daimler gasoline engine, used to tow a 15-in howitzer.

supplies because the available transport had been commandeered for the comforts and even the families of the officer corps.

The science of keeping troops supplied in the field is called logistics, and in various periods of history, logistics have been a highly developed and highly significant science, allowing the great generals to make best use of relatively small forces to inflict crushing defeats on their enemies through a combination of mobility and good physical condition. Logistics were, of course, aided by the development of good road systems, and a major boost was provided by the development of railroads. The latter provided the chance for large quantities of men and matériel to be moved long distances at high speed, and the effect of the railroads on military thinking were felt as early as the Civil War (1861-65) and the Franco-Prussian War (1870-71). From an early date, the nations of the European mainland were aware of the effect that railroads could have on European wars, and their governments

The ultimate means of battlefield movement in World War I was provided by the tank, which was a British invention designed to overcome obstacles such as barbed wire and machine gun strongpoints. This is a Tank Mk IV Female, which was armed with machine guns to provide gun-armed Tank Mk IV Male vehicles with protection against infantry attack, and which also carried an unditching beam to extricate itself from muddy areas, and a fascine (bundle of rods) to drop into trenches and so provide a crossing point.

thus moved readily into the control of how their national railroad networks spread: private enterprise was welcomed as a means of offsetting cost, but the governments made sure that national military and economic interests were served in the creation of new routes. The Germans raised the science of rail mobility to its peak in the period up to the outbreak of World War I.

In the Russo-Japanese War of 1904-5, Japan's military planners appreciated that their army was completely outnumbered by that of Imperial Russia, but realized that the relatively small Russian forces in Korea and Manchuria could be overcome before large-scale reinforcements could be moved along the Trans-Siberian Railroad from western Russia.

While the railroads completely changed the nature of military transport in the regions behind a battle area, and so forced changes in the period's strategic doctrines of how to wage war, they could not move equipment right up to the front line. In this tactical situation, animal transport was still the only effective means. Supplies were moved by rail to massive dumps set up at the railheads, as close as possible to the front line, and then collected by animal transport

This is a French field ambulance of the World War I period. These vehicles could not move close to the tortured front-line areas because of their very poor cross-country mobility, but were vital in moving casualties from rear-area stations to base hospitals.

Right: The Minerva armored car was a relatively powerful touring automobile, fitted with armor plate and armed with an 8-mm Hotchkiss machine gun above the crew compartment.

columns for onward movement to the fighting men. The railroads could also deliver additional men, but once they had reached the rail-head, the only means of movement to the front was still the soldier's age-old standby: his feet.

Change had been in the air, though, since the development of the automotive steam engine, and later the internal-combustion engine. Once the steam engine had been developed for railroad use as the steam locomotive, it was only a comparatively short step to its road equivalent, the steam traction engine. This, in fact, found its most

useful employment as a farm tractor, but was also used on roads for the movement of heavy loads. The weight of the traction engine was a hindrance to agility and speed, but provided excellent towing capabilities, which prompted army officers to consider the type as a heavy gun tractor. The Industrial Revolution, which had allowed the development of powerful steam engines, had also permitted the creation of heavy artillery, able to fire enormous shells over great ranges, but these pieces of ordnance were all but impossible to move, even with large teams of horses or oxen. When the guns were emplaced, they could only be used to good effect if they could be fed with a constantly renewed supply of ammunition. The traction engine was adopted to this task, for it had adequate pulling strength to tow heavy artillery and the limbers for the ammunition. The traction engine was inevitably slow, and therefore something of a tactical liability, but officers reasoned that heavy artillery was unlikely to have to decamp in a great hurry. Since heavy artillery was used only in limited quantities up to the beginning of World War I, the number of traction engines bought was comparatively small.

Traction engines were in themselves something of an evolutionary 'dead end,' however, because even in their fully-developed forms, they were limited by their considerable size, ponderous performance, and need for large quantities of coal and water. In the last 15 years of the 19th century, the internal-combustion engine made great developmental strides, from its very simple and limited beginnings to a position of useful power and adequate reliability. By comparison with the steam engine, the internal-combustion engine offered a far supe-

This is a Bussing mobile workshop of the type used by the German army in World War I. The vehicle is depicted here with its sides in the lowered positions in which they served as work platforms that could be adjusted in height relative to the ground, to provide stable and level 'floors' for the crew using the machinery installed on the truck bed.

Opposite below: A British experimental vehicle of the World War II period was this Armstrong Siddeley B10 tractor, a cross-country type designed for maximum capability with eight-wheel drive and an articulated chassis providing the ability to deal with terrain that differed in height laterally as well as longitudinally.

The Steyr-Daimler-Puch 1500 A was one of the German army standard 1.5-ton trucks in World War II. The design was from the drawing board of Dr. Ferdinand Porsche, and all four wheels were driven for moderately good cross-country mobility.

rior power-to-weight ratio, while demanding less in terms of fuel and water.

Many of the world's armies had moved into mechanization before World War I, but their main transport requirements were still met by animals. The effect of this reliance was felt in the first days of the war. Germany's strategic scheme was the 'Schlieffen Plan' that called for the right wing of Germany's advancing armies to sweep around to the west of the French capital, Paris, before turning south and then east to trap the Allied armies. But the distance was just too great for the German formation, which was exhausted and had to turn south before reaching Paris. This alteration resulted in Germany's initial defeat of the war at the first Battle of the Marne, in which the Allies made extensive use of motor transport (including English buses and Parisian taxicabs) to ferry fresh reinforcements to the battlefront.

After this, each side tried unsuccessfully to outflank the other to the north, this so-called 'race to the sea' resulting in the creation of the unmoving front line between the English Channel coast and the Swiss frontier that dominated the rest of the war. The front line was fortified on each side with semi-permanent trench lines, barbed wire, and machine gun positions.

Farther back from the front line, each side built up great stocks of the artillery which the generals regarded as the only means to defeat the enemy's artillery and destroy the barbed wire and machine gun defenses of the front line. Then, the generals hoped, the infantry could storm through the enemy's front line defenses and create a gap through which horse cavalry could advance and so inflict a war-winning defeat.

It did not happen this way and, with hindsight, it is possible to appreciate that it could never have happened with the transport and concepts available in the first part of World War I. As a result, the war stagnated. Vast offensives gained the victor a few hundred yards at the cost of hundreds of thousands of men. Even in this grim scenario, transport had its part to play. The front-line soldiers were served by foot, or at best by animal transport, but slightly farther behind the front, there buzzed increasingly large fleets of motorcycles for dispatch riders, ambulances, supply trucks, staff cars, and more specialized vehicles. These last became enormously important in the course of the 'Great War' as they offered unglamorous, but absolutely vital, services such as water purification and delousing, as well as a miscellany of repair facilities. Trucks were also used on an increasing scale to ferry ammunition to the gun lines, though the static nature of the war meant that the larger guns could be served by small railroads laid especially for the purpose.

The same pattern of static warfare was followed on other fronts such as those in Italy between the Italians and the Austro-Hungarians; in the Dardanelles (Gallipoli) between the Turks and the Allies (Australians, British, and New Zealanders), and in the Balkans between the Bulgarians and the Allies. Operations of a more mobile nature developed on the Eastern Front between the Russians and the Central Powers (Germany and

Opposite: An experimental Crossley tractor tested by the British with Kegresse half-tracks.

Austria-Hungary); in the Middle East between the Turks and the British; and in East Africa between the Germans and the various Allied nations. Some motor transport was used on the Eastern Front, but here the mainstays were draft animals and marching men. The East Africa campaign was one of marching infantry with comparatively small numbers of animals, but the Middle Eastern campaigns of Mesopotamia and Palestine saw more extensive use of motor transport. There was still extensive use of animals in both their draft and ridden forms (the latter including camels as well as horses and mules), but mechanized vehicles played an increasingly important part in mobile operations, and prophesied the way in which mobile operations would develop in World War II. Long, enveloping movements were made to cut off and trap the Turkish armies; infantry was carried in trucks and supported by truck-drawn artillery, while armored cars were used for deep reconnaissance and for attacks on

The German equivalent of the US Jeep in World War II was the excellent Kubelwagen. It was based on the Volkswagen automobile. It is seen here fitted with an optional propeller/rudder unit which was driven by the standard engine to provide amphibious capability.

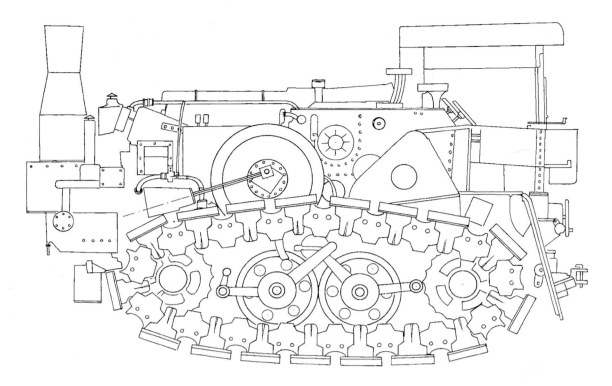

the Turks' rear areas and lines of communication. Undertaken in the heat, dust, and difficult terrain of the Middle East, these operations were important in proving that mechanized vehicles could cope with the extreme conditions of war.

Mechanization also reached the Western Front in France during 1916, in the form of the tank, but this falls outside the scope of this book as it was a weapon rather than a means of transport. In 1918, the final Allied victory was at last ensured by the British victory in the Battle of Amiens (August 8, 1918), but the breakthrough made possible by this success was exploited by the conventional transport of the Western Front rather than by masses of motor transport.

In the years immediately after World War I, the Allies were too exhausted, both spiritually and financially, to attempt any but the most superficial development of ideas that proved useful in the 'Great War.' During the course of

Left: The major impediments to movement on the battlefields of World War I on the Western Front were each side's defensive network of machine gun strongpoints and barbed wire, which proved insuperable to infantry and cavalry alike, and finally prompted the development of the tank. This soon proved itself to be the answer to the machine guns and barbed wire, but it was not the whole solution to battlefield mobility, for the years of war and constant artillery bombardment had transformed the countryside into a cratered wilderness, often flooded in winter, that could not be crossed by the transport vehicles of the day. One solution considered as a means of restoring transport mobility to the battlefield: was a steam-powered track-laying tractor, with modest climbing capability and the ability to tow guns or sleds loaded with men and/or supplies.

Below left: The World War II equivalent to the vehicle above, although fully realized and, as such, the precursor of the modern armored personnel carrier, was the half-track carrier. The trackwork provided the ability to cross all but the most inhospitable terrain, the steerable front wheels improved mobility and road speed, and the combination of tracks and wheels reduced cost by shortening the amount of track needed, together with its expensive road wheels, suspension, track-return rollers etc. This German vehicle is an SdKfz 251 half-track carrier equipped as a communications center for use by senior commanders of the XIX Corps.

The humble truck was one of the most important vehicles of World War II, for without huge fleets of such vehicles the support systems for the field armies would soon have ground to a halt. Most military trucks were of the 4 x 4 or 6 x 6 type for improved traction under adverse road conditions and, to a more limited extent, for a modest measure of cross-country capability. This is a Bedford truck of the British army.

Below: Considerable efforts were made during World War II to improve the mobility of all types of troops, including airborne forces who were by their very nature intended to operate beyond the conventional logistic support of their armies. Gliders were designed for the delivery of light vehicles such as Jeeps and even specially created light tanks, and this illustration depicts another innovation, namely a folding motorcycle for the use of British paratroops.

the late 1920s and early 1930s, however, the more far-sighted armies decided that full mechanization was the true path forward in purely military terms: the two most significant were the American and British armies, which launched ambitious schemes to replace all their animals, with the very limited exception of mules in such specialized tasks as jungle and mountain warfare. Henceforward, it was planned, the infantry would ride in trucks or, in the case of American soldiers in the battle zone, in half-tracked armored personnel carriers that combined the advantages of the truck in terms of cheapness and simplicity, and of the tracked vehicle in terms of cross-country mobility. Trucks were improved in their size, load-carrying capability, reliability, and versatility with more powerful engines, more flexible transmissions, and drive to all four or six wheels for better mobility in true cross-country operations; and considerable ingenuity went into the creation of truck-mounted services that could follow the infantry and satisfy all their battlefield needs.

It was planned that the motorized and mechanized infantry should operate with armored forces to create combined-arms teams. The motorized infantry was to be carried in trucks and supported by light and medium artillery of the truck-mounted type, while the mechanized infantry was to be carried in armored personnel carriers and supported by light and medium artillery of the self-propelled type mounted on a tracked chassis. The British and Soviets led the way with the creation of motorized infantry, while the American forces

Military Motorcycles

From its earliest times at the end of the 19th century, the motorcycle has offered lower purchase and operating costs than the automobile, together with a generally higher power/weight ratio and thus a superior capacity to handle difficult conditions that might cause an automobile to become bogged down. It was these factors that first attracted the military to the motorcycle, for the type was clearly ideal for the use of dispatch riders under wartime battlefield conditions as well as peacetime road conditions, and in the form of a sidecar combination, was attractive for alternative roles such as liaison and, in armed form, for fast reconnaissance and other more overtly offensive tasks.

One of the first recorded armed motorcycles was the unauthorized modification of a Harley-Davidson machine effected in 1908 by Sergeant Northover of the Canadian Militia, and comprised a standard motorcycle fitted with a modified sidecar containing a Vickers machine gun fixed to fire directly forward. At the time nothing came of the idea, but it was later adopted by most modern armies.

Typical of the type of armed motorcycle developed in world War I was the Vickers-Clyno Machine Gun Combination that appeared in 1915 for use by the Motor Machine Gun Corps, which received several hundreds of these equipments. The type was

based on the advanced Clyno motorcycle with a 5/6-hp engine driving the rear wheels by means of a three-speed gearbox and an enclosed drive. This was fitted with a sidecar carrying the tripod-mounted 0.303-in Vickers machine gun, a seat for the gunner, ammunition and spare cooling water for the gun as well as gasoline and oil for the motorcycle engine.

As German military strength was revived in the mid-1930s, mechanization was a key element of the process. Germany's industry's could not keep pace with demand for trucks and other mechanized vehicles, however, and considerable emphasis was therefore placed on the more easily produced motorcycle, of which the two most important makes in military service were the BMW and Zundapp with 750-cc engines and provision for a sidecar with a powered wheel.

Another fascinating German vehicle of a type allied to the motorcycle was the SdKfz 2 Kettenkrad, which was built by NSU as a tricycle type with twin tracked units in place of the rear wheels. The type was originally intended as a tractor for the use of airborne forces, and with a 1,500-cc engine could carry the driver and two rear-facing passengers at 50 mph, and could tow a load of 1,100 lb.

Below: A general inspects part of the Motor Machine Gun Corps in June 1918.

Opposite top: A section of the Motor Machine Gun Corps in training during February 1916, their equipment being motorcycle sidecar combinations each carrying a 0.303-in Vickers machine gun.

Opposite center: The Simms Quadricycle of 1898 was a private-venture British development with a 0.303in Maxim gun, and was decidedly ahead of its time in concept if not in its execution.

Opposite bottom: Seen in August 1941, a British army motorcycle combination carrying 0.303in Lewis machine gun. It was seen as one of several methods to combat and defeat German airborne invasion before the scattered paratroops could link up with each other.

Left: The US Army had been a firm believer in the military advantages of mechanization throughout this century. During World War II, the US army's field forces were very well supplied with motor transport of all types, with trucks featuring strongly for the movement of men and supplies. This General Motors 6 x 6 vehicle is typical of the breed, its powered paired rear wheel sets providing good traction even in muddy and generally slippery conditions.

Below: The USA also evolved the amphibious tractor, or Landing Vehicle Tracked, from experimental swamp vehicles of the period leading up to World War II. Driven in the water by cleats on their tracks, these vehicles were vital to the succes

were more ambitious and pushed forward with the creation of mechanized infantry.

This reflected industrial capability in addition to military thinking. The British and Soviets had well-advanced truck industries that could turn their attention, without undue cost or delay, to highly reliable load carriers with adequate cross-country performance. The Americans, on the other hand, saw the advantages of using their dynamic truck industry to create, for the mechanized infantry, the more expensive personnel carriers that provided superior cross-country mobility as well as protection for the embarked infantry.

The Americans were fortunate that World War II was two years further away from them than for the European nations; the delay allowed the development and production of the classic M2 and M3 series of half-track carriers, developed into a host of unarmed and armed forms in the war, and which have

Right: The most famous light transport of World War II was without doubt the Jeep, a 4 x 4 vehicle that was used for a host of tasks including armed reconnaissance with the type of armament depicted here, namely a pedestal-mounted 0.5-in Browning heavy machine gun. The Jeep was formidably reliable, could ford through moderately deep water, had good range and speed, and could also tow a sizable trailer if required.

Below: The German equivalent of the Jeep was the Kübelwagen, which was based on the chassis and automotive system of the Volkswagen automobile. The model seen here it fitted with a 0.312-in MG 34 machine gun.

been kept in service by a number of armies right up to the 1990s.

Oddly enough, given their successes in the first campaigns of World War II, the Germans were not as highly motorized or mechanized as most of their adversaries. The success of the German Blitzkrieg tactics against Poland, the Low Countries and France, Yugoslavia, Greece and, initially, the USSR, has produced the legend that masses of German tanks thundered forward, followed by hordes of motorized and/or mechanized infantry, supported by truck-towed artillery. This was not the case, for the Germans were late into the field of army mechanization, and until 1941, were still reliant mainly on draft animals. The Panzer divisions were supported by artillery, sometimes towed by trucks or, in the case of heavier equipment, by tracked towing vehicles rather than draft animals; but they were very poorly supported by the infantry, which generally had to march. The German victories were good ideas turned into brilliant practice, but a careful reading of World War II history reveals that the German plans frequently came close to disaster when the

Above: The White M3 4 x 4 truck was a personnel carrier of World War II with accommodation for the driver and up to seven passengers, and was lightly armored for protection on the battlefield. Over 20,000 of these vehicles were delivered, and the type was later developed into the class M3 series of half-track carriers. The roller at the front was designed to help the vehicle to extricate itself from ditched positions.

Panzer divisions outpaced the weary infantry, and had to wait in dangerously exposed positions for the support to catch up.

On the Allied side, especially in the American camp, World War II witnessed the real blossoming of military transport. From 1943 onward, the Allied advances relied ever more heavily on tracked and wheeled vehicles for the supplies and the mobility that enabled them to grind down the still formidable German fighting machine. As in World War I, there were vehicles for all purposes, but the availability of more and better vehicles allowed ingenious military planners to devise more an increasing range of specialized vehicles to ease the task of the fighting men. There were, of course, the standard types, such as motorcycles for the urgent movement of messages in the absence of radio or telephone communication, supply trucks, artillery tractors, ambulances, and staff cars. But in addition to the half-track (which was also used by the Germans to a more limited extent), World War II saw the widespread adoption of vehicles such as the jeep, amphibious tractor (often called amtrack or amphtrack), and tank transporter. As Winston Churchill said "Victory is the beautiful bright-coloured flower; transport is the stem, without which it could never have blossomed."

Many attempts were made between the 1930s and the 1950s to design a cost-effective vehicle combining the cross-country mobility of the tracked vehicle with the mechanical simplicity and load-carrying capability of the standard truck, but most such projects foundered on insuperable problems of weight, complexity and cost.

It is impossible to overstate the importance of the Willys Jeep, an exceptional little vehicle of sturdy construction. Its one real problem was the poor protection offered to the crew in bad weather; but in all military respects, the jeep was a superb vehicle with a rugged engine, four-wheel drive, and a high ground clearance to provide a good combination of road and cross-country performance, with the ability to ford modestly deep water without preparation. These are the hallmarks of the true military transport, and the jeep

had them all in good measure despite its small overall size. The jeep was used for all manner of tasks ranging from communications to scouting, via front-line supply and casualty evacuation. Other nations had their equivalents, and that which came closest in performance and capability to the American vehicle was the German Kübelwagen, based on the chassis and automotive system of the Volkswagen car. But the Germans could never match the Americans for production, so their Kubelwagen was less important in overall terms. American production was vast, allowing the jeep to be issued on a lavish scale to US forces, and almost on as generous a scale to many of the Allied forces.

The DUKW (pronounced 'duck') was designed in 1942 by General Motors in collaboration with the yacht designers Sparkman & Stevens, as a ruck suitable for amphibious operations. The DUKW could be driven into the water from ramp-equipped ships, or lowered by crane, thereafter shuttling between ships and inland dumps with

Above and below: Modern personnel carriers, such as these vehicles seen in United Nations markings for service in the so-called peacekeeping operation in the former Yugoslavia during the 1990s, often have an 8 x 8 wheeled drive that combines modest cost with good cross-country mobility, an armored hull with access to troop compartment via power-operated ramp/door at the rear, and provision for defensive and, to an increasing extent, offensive armament.

5,000lb of supplies or 25 troops. The DUKW was liable to swamping in all but calm water, but proved itself to be of immense value in amphibious operations, such as those which took the Allied armies ashore in Italy and France during 1943 and 1944 respectively; and it played a prominent part in major river-crossing operations, such as that to ferry the Allies across the River Rhine and into the heart of Germany during April 1945. In the water, the DUKW was steered by a rudder and driven by its propeller at 5.5 knots; on land, it became a conventional six-wheel drive vehicle with a maximum speed of

50mph. Other nations attempted similar vehicles, but none was as successful as the DUKW.

The amphibious tractor was more properly called the Landing Vehicle Tracked (LVT), and was designed to provide much the same capability as the DUKW, with the added advantage of cleated tracks that provided waterborne propulsion as well as a superior ability to climb over reefs and up difficult shores. The LVT underwent intensive development in World War II, and was successively

This is a modern 6 x 6 armored personnel carrier with a rotating turret to provide the vehicle commander with the ability to see right round his machine while remaining under cover. The turret also carries armament.

fitted with features such as a ramp so that it could be used to land troops for assault landings, armor protection, machine gun armament and, in later models, offensive armament in the form of a light tank turret or a 75mm howitzer. Production was extensive, and the importance of the type to the American effort against the Japanese in the Pacific was enormous. The type was also used in Europe against the Germans, and as with the DUKW, there were never enough of these excellent vehicles to meet demand.

The Allies' extensive employment of amphibious assault operations also demanded the creation of specialized vehicles such as beach armored recovery vehicles, which were tanks stripped of their arma-

As has always been the case, armies today are wholly dependent on the arrival of food and clean water for drinking purposes. Although most modern armies equip their men with tablets that will sterilize unclean water, a better solution is the use of water tankers such as those seen here.

ment and fitted with deep wading equipment, to allow their use as wreckers on beaches where bogged-down or disabled vehicles could cause a disastrous delay in the flow of men and equipment off the assault beach.

The role of the tank transporter is self-evident. It was designed for the rapid movement of tanks over long distances, so that the short-lived tracks on the tanks would not be unduly worn by to slow churning along roads and across country. The availability of tank transporters also afforded the tank forces greater operational mobility, allowing substantial armored forces to appear where the enemy least expected them.

Other vehicle types, such as bulldozers and combat engineer tractors, were developed and placed into service, albeit in smaller numbers. In World War II, many tanks, especially of the older types that were approaching obsolescence in their primary gun tank role, were fitted with a hydraulically operated bulldozer blade that allowed their use for the creation of beach and river bank gradients, the establishment of level positions for the artillery, and the quick erection of dirt barriers. Military conversions of civilian bulldozers were also used, and both types have been further developed since World War II. The tank fitted with a blade does not lose much in mobility or speed, and can quickly create for itself a dug-in position that leaves only the turret and its main gun exposed to view. Designated bulldozers pro-

The US Army's modern equivalent to the Jeep is the "Hummer", which is the semi-acronymic name derived from the vehicle's real designation, which is the HMMWV (High-Mobility Multi-Purpose Wheeled Vehicle). This is a 4 x 4 type with a General Motors V-8 diesel engine of 6,200-cc capacity for a maximum road speed of 65 mph and a maximum road range of 351 miles after departure at a maximum weight of 8,532 lb. The "Hummer" is generally used as a light transport, but there are many variations on this basic theme including an anti-tank vehicle armed with the Hughes BGM-71 TOW heavyweight missile system.

Right and below: The "Hummer" possesses good fording and all-terrain capability without the limits of its long chassis and 4 x 4 drive, and had demonstrated impressive reliability under most conditions of terrain and climate. The type's most important 'failing,' is its comparatively modest range, although this is a relatively insignificant factor under all but the most exceptional of circumstances. One of the important advantages offered by diesel-engined propulsion is the use of a low-volatility fuel that does not ignite as readily as gasoline: this has obvious advantages for a battlefield vehicle likely to be hit by enemy fire.

vide the same capability as their World War II forerunners, but with greater speed and agility. From these two basic types evolved the combat engineer tractor, a vehicle fitted with specialist equipment, such as an earth auger, bulldozer blade, winch, jib crane, and demolition gun. To provide maximum protection for the crew, these combat engineer tractors are almost always based on the chassis and hull of main battle tanks, which gives them much the same performance as the tank forces they are designed to support.

Since World War II, no radically new military transport concepts heve evolved. Emphasis has been placed on developing the notions explored and proved in World War II. The global nature of modern warfare, for example, has promoted the development of freight and personnel transports suitable for use in a wide variety of climates and terrain. At the same time, the needs of the most extreme conditions have been met by the creation of highly specialized types such as snowmobiles and swamp-crossers: the former are in fairly extensive service, but the latter are still largely experimental.

Modern military vehicles are mechanically more advanced than the vehicles of World War II, with features such as automatic transmission and high-technology suspension. The gasoline engine has given way almost completely to the diesel with its more readily available fuel, lower risk of fire, and higher range for a given volume of fuel. Complementing this internal development are three external tendencies that are more readily apparent in the development of modern military transport: tactical versatility, enclosed accommodation (to provide protection against nuclear, biological, and chemical warfare agents), and measures to improve cross-country mobility.

No matter what other vehicles are designed and adopted for use by armed forces, the basic truck remains wholly indispensable to every army in the world.

Tactical versatility has been enhanced by basing modern transports on a core chassis and automotive system that can be built up as several types of specialized vehicle, or alternatively fitted with a flatbed onto which can be lowered a palletized or containerized system that fits the vehicle to the desired role. For example, palletized freight can be moved on one trip, and then the vehicle's flatbed can be fitted with a containerized communications system with its own power supply. Enclosed accommodation offers protection against some of the effects of NBC (nuclear, biological and chemical) warfare. Filters are used to remove harmful agents, and the accommodation also provides air conditioning and temperature control.

Mobility has been increased in both wheeled and tracked transports. In more advanced armies, there has been a move toward comparatively light aluminum bodies on fully tracked vehicles with their inherently superior cross-country mobility, and there has also been considerable development of six- and eight-wheel drive wheeled vehicles, whose mobility is not inferior to that of tracked vehicles, but which are much cheaper to develop and produce, and also considerably easier to maintain. These last are of great importance to the developing countries that are the main market for these wheeled vehicles. It is difficult to forsee any further short-term roles that can be undertaken by military transports, but the future will certainly witness further improvements in performance and utility.

Sea Transportation

Sailing Ships

ailing ships are among the most beautiful things ever made by man. In the Western world, we now know them mostly as yachts and as larger ships, preserved as museums or sail training ships, but in many other parts of the world they are still practical and effective working vessels. In such sailing ships, men travel lakes, rivers, shallow coastal waters, and deep oceans for trade, transport, and fishing. Indeed, it is difficult to see how most Third World countries could survive without ships and boats powered by the wind, which is free, and in many parts of the world blows with great regularity. The industrial countries may no longer have to rely on the wind for power, but it is still vitally important in poorer and less industrialized countries that do not have the money and skills to import and operate the internal-combustion engines that we in the West take for granted.

Up to 150 years ago, when the age of steam began to produce practical and reliable coal-fired engines, the wind was the only alternative to muscle power for the movement of both large ships and small boats. Even after the arrival of the steam engine, it was a long time before sailing ships became obsolete for everything except pleasure. The steam engine, fired by coal and then by oil, first had to prove itself in reliability and economy while driving paddle wheels and then propellers, and it was the beginning

With their rounded hull, curved fore and after ends, steering rudder, single square sail, and high fore- and aftercastles, early warships were poor sailers on anything but a run before the wind. The fore- and aftercastles were designed as platforms for the embarked archers to shoot into enemy ships before the vessels were grappled together and a miniature land battle was fought for overall possession.

of the 20th century before sail really gave way to steam. For perhaps 6,000 years before that, sailing ships were among man's most important designs. It would be pleasant to think that we 'invented' sailing, but from the beginning of time, leaves have been blown across puddles, bugs across ponds, and branches down rivers by the power of the wind. And it is thought that the wind, working with the waves, was responsible for the migration of many plants, insects, and even animals from the mainlands to many island groups. At some unknown time, a man must have imagined that he could rig a primitive mast and sail (probably a pole and a fur) onto a straight log to capture the wind's power, and steer his creation with his arms or a paddle. Such a primitive sailing craft would have been able to cross wide rivers and perhaps even small lakes, but would have been unable to steer very far from the way the wind was blowing.

By comparison with the square sail, the lateen sail offered the great advantage of allowing the vessel to sail far closer to the wind and to tack through the eye of the wind with considerably greater ease. Moreover, the fact that this triangular sail could be drawn round athwartships meant that the lateen-sailed vessel could also run before the wind with modest efficiency.

Man the inventor was soon improving this primitive system. It is thought that, by 4000 BC the Chinese were using sail-driven rafts, a model of a sailing boat used on the Tigris and Euphrates rivers has been dated by archaeologists at about 3500 BC, and by 3400 BC the Egyptians were using sailing craft on rivers. Before long, the Egyptians had begun to trade along their coast and across the Mediterranean by

Left and below: The galley, seen left, and below in its Venetian ceremonial and fighting forms, was much favored for operations in Mediterranean waters as masts could be stepped and sails set when the wind was advantageous, but otherwise oar power could be used for continued movement and, in battle, for the type of agility that could not be matched by any pure sailing vessel. The primary limitations on the use of such vessels were their very large complement and resulting requirement for food and water, and their high length/beam ratio. The former meant that only short voyages could be undertaken, and the latter resulted in poor performance in all but relatively calm waters.

sailing ship. Most river boats were probably made of reed bundles lashed together to make a hull with a wide and stable central section and a pointed bow and stern, which were lifted out of the water by special lashings or by a central rope connecting the bow and stern. Just in front of the central position, a short mast was placed (or stepped) with rope bracings (or stays) to the bow and stern, with more bracings (or shrouds) to the sides of the hull formed by the reed bun-

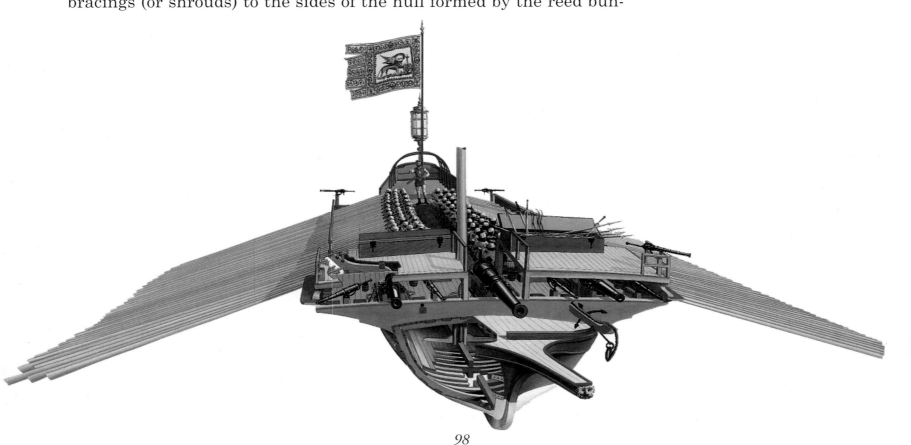

dles. These stays and shrouds held the mast upright and allowed it to carry a square sail hanging from a stout yard. The yard was controlled by rope braces running to the stern of the boat, and the bottom of the sail by further lines (sheets). Steering was entrusted to a large paddle-bladed oar, lashed to hang down into the water beside or behind the stern.

Sailing ships designed for trips more than a short distance from the coast were built to the same basic pattern, but they were larger and, whenever possible, made of wood rather than reed. The Egyptians did not have the type of tree that would provide long planks, so they used short planks (generally thick enough to be regarded as blocks) pinned together and made watertight by a wadding (or caulking) of papyrus reed hammered into the gaps, and painted over with pitch or tree resin to make it more water-resistant. The square sail was suitable only to make the ship move directly in front of the wind or slightly away from this direction, so ships were generally fitted for oars as an alternative to sails when the wind failed or was blowing from the wrong direction. The oars were also important in maneuvering the ship in harbors. They were clumsy craft, but they worked and allowed countries such as Egypt to develop as important trading nations.

The sailing ship was also developed for fighting, and it is thought likely that this led to the development of 'clewing.' On the earliest ships, the spar and sail were lowered to the deck by a rope halliard when not needed. On a trading ship this was acceptable, but the long yard and large sail would have been in the way of the soldiers. For this reason, therefore, it was arranged for the yard to remain at the top of the mast with the sail lifted (or clewed) up against it, where it was firmly furled when not needed. It is thought that this development evolved on the northern shore of the Mediterranean. It was only a short step from clewing to the development of reef points, which are rows of short lines sewn into the

Above: The adoption of a two-masted layout allowed a greater area of sail to be carried, which offered the possibility of considerably improved performance.

Below: This is a depiction of the carrack type of vessel in its early form with square sails on the fore and main masts and a lateen sail on the mizzen mast.

99

Left: This vessel shows the development of the basic sail plan with head sails, main, and top sails on the fore, and main masts, and a lateen-rigged mizzen mast. This combination gave the vessel the ability to sail both on and off the wind. The adoption of two sails on each of the two forward masts allowed the quantity of sail set to be varied to suit the wind strength and direction without any need for reefing.

sail so that they can be tied around the yard once the sail had been lifted slightly, as a means of reducing the amount of sail offered to a rising wind. The use of several rows allowed exactly the right area of sail to be furled as required.

Unlike the Egyptians, the Phoenicians of the Levant coast (now Lebanon and Israel) had suitable wood, in the form of Lebanese cedar, for long planks for their merchant ships, which resembled Egyptian ships in shape. The use of longer planks allowed the Phoenicians to make stronger ships that could sail farther from the coast and brave worse weather. Therefore, they could undertake longer voyages, which possibly included, it is thought, a three-year expedition around Africa in the 7th century BC. The Phoenicians were also the first to develop a ship especially for war. It was a narrow type that could be sailed before any favorable wind, but which was fitted with one, two, or even three banks of oars for

Below: This three-masted lateen rig on a large hull was typical of the trading vessels that plied the Mediterranean. With most of the power generated by the largest sail on the forward-raked fore mast but balanced by the smaller sails located farther aft, the vessels could be handled with safety by a comparatively small and therefore economical crew.

Built as a collier but brought into the Royal Navy as HMS *Endeavour* for Captain James Cook's first great voyage of exploration (1768-71) into the South Seas, this ship was of very sturdy construction and possessed capacious holds, which was rightly considered essential for a vessel that would have to carry an enormous quantity of stores of all kinds. The *Endeavour* was a 366-ton barque with ten 4-pounder carriage guns and 12 swivel guns.

speed and maneuverability in naval battles. Despite these important developments, the Phoenicians lacked the engineering skill to make ships that were notably larger than those of the Egyptians. It was the Greeks, and to a larger extent, the Romans, who built the Western world's first large ships after developing the idea of a large and very strong frame on which was laid an arrangement of caulked planks to provide a watertight hull.

Below: The cutter was introduced in the middle of the 18th century as a single-masted decked vessel with good performance to windward as a result of its fore-and-aft sails, and adequate downwind performance with the aid of its square sails. The type was much used for coastal patrol and the delivery of dispatches.

The Romans were responsible for the creation of what can be called the modern sailing ship. The Roman structure was based on a strong keel running from bow to stem, where uprights called the stern and sternpost rose to give the ship strength against the buffeting of the waves. The shape of the hull was given by large frames rising from the keel, and held in place by the stringers that ran in wide curves from the stem to the sternpost. Over this frame was laid the hull planking and the deck sections to create a large, hollow interior.

The system allowed the building of larger, as well as more seaworthy ships, and this in turn opened the way for tub-like merchantmen and sword-like fighting ships. The one- or two-masted merchantmen were wide and slow, but were well suited to the task of carrying the bulk of Rome's

Above and below left: The frigate was the made-of-all-work of most navies in the 18th and early 19th centuries. Seen (above) with sweeps rigged for movement in the absence of wind, the frigate generally carried between 24 and 38 guns on a single deck, and was notable for sailing qualities very considerably superior to those of line-of-battle ships.

enormous trade. The warships were fast and maneuverable, and the use of clewed sails allowed them to sail rapidly into battle. Enemy ships were rammed with the warship's long reinforced bow and left to sink, or boarded and captured by soldiers who were carried for just this purpose.

The Roman shipbuilders used planks laid side-by-side (carvel construction) to produce a smooth finish next to the water. This basic structure and finish was standard across Europe until the decline of the Roman empire in the 5th century AD. It remained the most widely used method of shipbuilding in the Mediterranean after this time, but as Roman influence in northern Europe waned, the Roman techniques were largely lost.

The powerful new seafarers in northern Europe were the Viking people from Scandinavia. The Vikings pioneered a new type of sailing ship, usually known as the longship. It was used for coastal and ocean voyages under sail or oar power, and was designed as a capacious ship

Right: Perhaps the single most celebrated ship ever to have served with the US Navy, the USS *Constitution* was one of the "six original frigates" authorized by the Congress and launched in 1797. This ship, now berthed in Boston as a floating monument, was of 2,200 tons displacement and carried 44 guns. The ship was instrumental in raising US morale during the War of 1812, when she defeated and destroyed the 48-gun British frigate HMS *Guerriére*, whose shot failed to penetrate the *Constitution*'s hull. This led to the nickname "Old Ironsides" for a ship that later in her career defeated and destroyed the frigate HMS *Java* and in a separate action defeated and captured two smaller vessels, the 32-gun HMS *Cyane* and 20-gun HMS *Levant*.

Below: This cutaway view of a warship of the late 18th century reveals the main stowage for stores, water, cordage, spare sails and spars, ammunition and powder on the lower decks, while the upper decks accommodated the guns and men, the latter in conditions of great privation and discomfort.

with a flat bottom that did not penetrate far into the water, and that could be beached as well as brought alongside. This shallow-draft hull was well-suited to conditions in northern Europe: the Vikings could beach their ships for safety in the winter, and in the summer they used them to push deep into fjords and rivers on their raiding and trading voyages. The Viking ships were like those of the Phoenicians in being long and thin, but like those of the Romans in being built-up on a frame. Northern Europe had lost the technique of carvel planking, and the longships were clinker-built, with the lower edge of each plank overlapping the upper edge of the plank below it.

Driven before the wind by a single square sail or moved by its oars,

Left: The American *Heidi-9* is a typical ketch, a two-masted vessel with the mizzen mast stepped forward of the rudder post.

Below: Built in Germany by Blohm und Voss and commissioned in 1938 as the sail training ship *Albert Leo Schlageter*, this three-masted barque (square-rigged on the fore and main masts, and fore and aft-rigged on the mizzen mast) was seized by the USA after World War II and sold to Brazil as the *Guanabara*. She was bought by the Portuguese navy in 1972 and renamed *Sagres II,* and as seen here is a sister ship of the ex-*Horst Wessel* now operated by the US Coast Guard as the *Eagle*.

the longship was ideally suited to the Viking way of life. The Vikings also discovered that the yard could be braced far around, so that the sail was angled more to the hull than running across it, and this allowed the longship to sail crabwise into the general direction of the wind, in a zigzag maneuver known as 'tacking.' In their longships, these adventurous people traded through the rivers of eastern Europe to reach the Black Sea, sailed around the coasts of western Europe to enter the Mediterranean through the Straits of Gibraltar, and most impressively of all, sailed west into the Atlantic to discover and settle Iceland, Greenland, and even North America before 1000 AD.

As the northern Europeans began to come out of the Dark Ages that followed the fall of Rome, its seafaring peoples began to build up an important trade network using a small but stout ship that combined the layout of the Mediterranean ship (a fat hull with two or three masts) with the Viking type of clinker construction. The trade network grew rapidly up to about 1000 AD, and during this period oars generally disappeared from northern European

ships. Merchants were trying to save money by reducing the size of crews, while improved layout and skills meant that ships could more easily use the Viking-discovered ability of ships to sail into the general direction of the wind by bracing the yards around. Speed for its own sake was not important to traders, whose ships were therefore wide for their length, to increase their cargo-carrying capacity and make them simple to sail with small crews.

At much the same time, larger carvel-built merchant ships with two or three masts began to appear. Each one carried a single square sail on each of the masts, but as ships increased in size, the masts were lengthened by adding one or two more sections above the main mast, each section carrying its own sail in an arrangement that allowed exactly the right adjustment of sails for all weathers and conditions. Ships were becoming more maneuverable, and in the 12th century the sharply sloped stern began to disappear in favor of a more upright kind that could take a hinged rudder. With this development, the steering oar disappeared, and ships became not only easier, but also more precise to handle. The true rudder and square sails could be braced far around toward the side of the ship.

Together, they provided the ability to sail in any direction except directly into or close to the wind, and it was

Above: The *Amerigo Vespucci* is the largest of the Italian navy's sail training ships, and was commissioned in May 1931 as a ship-rigged vessel of 3,540-ton displacement. The ship is notable for her color scheme, specially selected to suggest the black-and-white arrangement of many warships in the first half of the 19th century.

Below: The design and layout of whaling ships was optimized for strength and capacity rather than sailing performance, and notable features were the large brick-built stove for the rendering of whale blubber, large holds for the barrels of whale oil, and the accommodation and stores for a crew who might be away from home, or indeed from any port, for a period of several years.

possible to make headway in these directions by tacking. This improvement marked the end of oared ships in northern Europe, where rough weather is common: but in the Mediterranean, oared warships remained in service until after the beginning of the 18th century.

The main types of trading ship employed in the Mediterranean in the period from the 14th to the 17th centuries were the caravel and the carrack, both built with considerable freeboard (hull height above the waterline). The caravel, the smaller of the two, was a boat-built type in which the forward-curving beakhead and the aftercastle of the northern European ships was replaced by a curved stem and a flat transom, more suitable to the calmer seas of the Mediterranean. These vessels were generally two-masted, with a single lateen (triangular fore-and-aft) sail on each mast, and were able to sail closer to the wind than the square-rigged north European vessels. The Spanish and Portuguese began to use the caravel in the 16th century ,and soon found that the lateen rig was not suitable for long ocean voyages. These two great exploring nations therefore developed the caravel into a three-masted type, with square sails on the two forward masts and a lateen-

Above: The *Pride of Baltimore* is typical of the type of vessel now used for sail and adventure training. The basically fore-and-aft schooner rig provides good sailing qualities and can be handled by a small crew, while the square sails provide improved downwind performance as well as the opportunity for the crew to learn to handle square sails.

Below: Sailors venturing into the vastness of oceans such as the Pacific were faced with the prospect of surviving on their own resources for very extended periods, and their ships were therefore well provided with stores and the equipment to mend or refashion all vital pieces of equipment.

rigged mizzen mast. The three ships of Christopher Columbus's voyage across the Atlantic in 1492 were caravels. The Santa Maria was a 95ft. vessel typical of larger caravels, while the Pinta and the Nina were 58ft. and 56ft. vessels typical of smaller caravels. The Nina started the voyage with 'caravela latina' rig, but this equipment was so difficult to control in the Atlantic that she was converted to the three-masted 'caravela rotunda' rig when the expedition reached the Canary Islands.

The carrack was the larger trading ship used in the Mediterranean and also in northern Europe between the 14th and 17th centuries, and was, in effect, a cross between the lateen-rigged Mediterranean ship and the square-rigged north European ship. It was thus similar to the fully developed caravel with three masts, but was larger and broader in the beam, with a displacement of up to 1,200 tons. The carrack was generally of sturdy construction, and carried fore- and aftercastles. The carrack was the first example of the 'typical' trading ship that lasted until the arrival of steam, with square-rigged fore and main masts, plus a lateen-rigged mizzen mast. The only real development of the carrack resulted in the galleon. This design eliminated the high forecastle with

The *Fantome* passes the cruise liner Rotterdam. The latter may possess all the comfortable attractions of a floating hotel, but lacks any of the dynamic beauty of any sailing vessel.

its tendency to blow the bow downwind, resulting in a ship that was able to sail closer to the wind.

Except for the lateen on the mizzen, ships were rigged with square sails until the middle of the 17th century. By this time, the lateen had begun to give way to the more manageable spritsail, which was rigged completely aft of the mast with a diagonal spar running from low on the mast to the rear upper corner of the spritsail. The evolution was completed when the spritsail was replaced by the four-sided spanker, or driver, with a boom at its foot and a gaff at its head.

The driver was initially considered a fair-weather sail, but its easy tacking meant that it finally replaced the lowest square sail on the mizzen (the mizzen course) after the middle of the 18th century.

Square-rigged ships work best when running before the wind, whereas ships with fore-and-aft rigs can sail closer to the wind. By the middle of the 17th century, serious efforts were being made to combine the two types of rig to produce a sailing ship able to move before or tack into the wind with equal ease. The mizzen spritsail was a move in the right direction, but greater capability came from the adoption

In its fully developed form, the three-masted ship was and is an extraordinarily complex machine, rescued from catastrophe by the masterly fashion in which all its cordage and other features are arranged to operate in their designed tasks, without interfering with other elements of the complete system.

of staysails and jibs. Staysails are triangular sails set on the stays that brace the masts against fore-and-aft movement, while the jibs, also triangular, are set on the stays bracing the foremast to the bowsprit, running forward from the bow and previously used for a spritsail (below) and a small square sail (above).

As trade increased in volume and importance during the 19th century, greater emphasis was placed on speed, as well as on smaller crews for higher profits. The handling of fore-and-aft rigs requires fewer men than square rigs, and ship designers combined the two basic types of rig in the ships of the period. The larger ships were the barque and the barquentine. The barque displaced up to 5,500 tons and had between three and five masts, of which the forward two were always square-rigged. The barquentine had three masts and was square-rigged only on the foremast. The smaller ships were the brig and brigantine. The brig is a two-masted ship square-rigged on both masts, while the brigantine is also two-masted, but square-rigged on only the foremast.

The ultimate in sailing vessels able to sail to windward is the schooner, which began to appear at the beginning of the 18th century

Right: The British aviation pioneer T.O.M. Sopwith was also a devotee of yacht racing, and with two *Endeavours* tried to wrest the America's Cup from the Americans during the 1930s. Both these yachts were J-class sloops designed by Charles Nicholson and built by the Camper and Nicholson yard, and in the last two race series Sopwith sailed in these boats before the introduction of the 12-meter class. *Endeavour I* was beaten by *Rainbow* in 1934 and *Endeavour II* by *Ranger* in 1937.

One of the ultimate sailing machines of its period, the American cutter *Reliance* carried a huge sail area on a small hull with an even shorter waterline length, and successfully defended the America's Cup in 1903 against the British *Shamrock III*, a cutter owned by Sir Thomas Lipton.

Below: Details of the deck plans and internal arrangement of the *Reliance*, which was designed on the 'skimming dish' principle with a fin keel, and as such was altogether faster than the more conventional British boat.

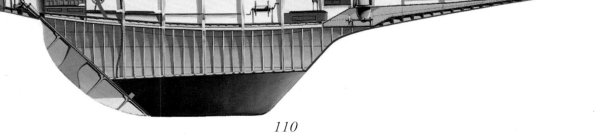

The 'wishbone' schooners that worked the cod fighting grounds of the Grand Banks off the eastern coast of Canada were some of the most impressive sailing vessels ever designed. The schooners were fast and weatherly, but could be handled with complete safety by a small crew. This is *Bluenose*, the fastest of all the 'wishbone' schooners and also a successful racing boat.

in Massachusetts as a fairly small, two- or three-masted vessel fore-and-aft rigged on all its masts. These were fast and extremely weatherly vessels, at first carrying four-sided main sails, but from the middle of the 18th century seen increasingly with the Bermudan rig, which replaces four-sided sails with triangular sails that have their heads at the top of the masts and so dispense with the gaff and all its rigging.

In the early medieval period, there was little need for naval warfare. When warships were needed, merchant ships loaded with men, rather than cargo, were used, and naval battles consisted of closing in on the enemy so that the soldiers could board and capture the enemy ships – in short, a land battle transferred onto the sea. But, with the arrival of gunpowder weapons in the 14th century, a change was forced. At first, warships could be adapted from merchant ships with their forecastles and poops fitted with light cannon, but as cannon became more common and larger in size, the ships became top heavy. So, warships became longer and lower, with the cannon arranged in broadside rows along the length of the upper deck. At the same time,

Among the last practical uses left for workaday sailing craft in the Western world was fishing, in which craft such as this Maldon boat from the English east coast could earn a living into the 1950s.

the forecastles and poops were made taller, so that light weapons could be mounted in and on them to attack the enemy ship's crew and, in the event that the ship was boarded, to shoot down into the enemy fighting in the waist of the ship between the forward and after 'castles.' The scheme worked well when the ships were involved in battle, but it made them difficult to sail, as the large area of the forecastle and poop allowed the wind to push the ship sideways.

The French *Gloire* was the first ironclad warship, and as such marked a turning point in naval matters. The ship was launched in 1859 and, in addition to her steam powerplant delivering 2,500 hp to a single four-blade propeller for a speed of 13 kt, was also rigged as a barque with square sails on her fore and main masts, and fore-and-aft sails on all three masts.

Right and below right: Since the beginning of the 1970s there had been a considerable growth in public interest about yacht racing, which is one of the few types of wind-powered activity still pursued on a very large scale. This general interest was matched by a determination in many countries to wrest the America's Cup, generally considered as the acme of match racing in day yachts, from the Americans who had held the trophy since 1851. This determination has spread from the UK, which for more than a century was the traditional challenger, to countries as diverse as Spain, France, Canada, Italy and Japan but including as the strongest, and ultimately only two successful, challengers in the forms of Australia and New Zealand. The efforts of these two countries are typified by the 12-meter class yachts *Australia* (above) and *New Zealand* (below).

These early warships were of about 500 tons, though some English warships were as large as 1,000 tons. Late in the 16th century, English shipbuilders began to develop warships with lower 'castles,' especially at the bow. These ships were so much better at sailing, that they could outmaneuver their enemies and use their guns in positions from which the enemy could not reply. Larger numbers of guns were installed by increasing the height of the hull and arranging the guns on separate decks. This English development was soon copied by other European navies to produce hard-hitting ships that could also sail well.

Racing in sailing boats is always an exciting experience, and one of the most exhilarating elements of racing in dinghies is the art of trapezing on a wire extending from a point high on the mast, so that a member of the crew can help to keep the boat as upright as possible.

This established the pattern of warships until well into the 19th century. Refinements were made, but the basic pattern remained unaltered, despite a growth in size to about 3,000 tons and 130 guns by the middle of the 19th century. The emphasis in warship design was on speed and agility, calling for a long, comparatively narrow hull, which improved the warship's ability to carry the long rows of guns needed to fire effective broadside salvos. By the middle of the 18th century, the increasing formality of naval warfare had led most navies to introduce special designations for their warships. Ships were designated, by the number of their guns, into six 'rates.' The first three, and sometimes the fourth, were 'line of battle ships,' while the fifth and sixth were frigates designed to scout for the heavier vessels. The exact number of guns that decided the rate varied slightly with date, but at the time of Lord Nelson's victory at the Battle of Trafalgar in 1805, a first-rate ship had more than 100 guns, a second-rate ship between 84 and 100, a third-rate ship between 70 and 84, a fourth-rate ship between 50 and 70, a fifth-rate ship between 32 and 50, and a sixth-rate ship less than 32. The need of the larger ships to accommodate the guns on up to three gundecks led to the development of warships that were comparatively tall. To reduce stability problems, the hulls were given great 'tumblehome,' the attractive inward curve of the hull above the point of greatest beam.

The heaviest guns were placed as low as possible to reduce stability problems still further, and the guns were fired through portholes in the hull that were covered by heavy port lids when the guns were not being used. The guns had long barrels and were extremely heavy, recoiling far inboard when fired and requiring heavy tackles to stop them from sliding. The recoil brought the muzzle inboard of the port lid, which allowed these muzzle-loading weapons to be reloaded without undue difficulty before being run out again to their firing positions. The effective range of naval cannon was only about 200 yards, so naval battles were generally side-by-side slugging matches in which weight of fire (the weight of the ball fired and the number of rounds fired) counted more than pinpoint accuracy; the largest cannon carried by first-rate ships fired a 42lb ball, and the lightest standard cannon fired an 18lb ball. The tendency toward weight of fire reached its height in the Napoleonic wars, when the carronade was introduced as a short-range 'smasher.' To reduce its recoil, this gun was mounted on a slide rather than wheels, and was a notably inaccurate weapon, designed to fire a large ball over a short range. Solid shot was designed to penetrate thick hull planking, and other projectiles were used to knock down masts, rigging, and men.

The warships led the way in the development of sailing techniques during the 15th, 16th, and 17th centuries. To move bulk cargoes at the lowest cost, merchant traders were still in favor of large hulls moved by two square sails on each of three masts, typical of the 250-ton caravel that was the most important trading ship until the end of the 14th century. But the opening of new transoceanic trade routes to the east and west as a result of the 'Age of Discovery' opened the way for larger and more weatherly ships, such as the Spanish high-forecastle carracks and their successors, the low-forecastle galleons of up to 1,600 tons. The merchant companies formed by most northern European countries to conduct the trade to India and the Far East, used another successor of the carrack, the East Indiamen. The development of this luxury trade began to place increasing emphasis on

Yacht racing poses immense strain on spars, rigging and sails deliberately made as flimsy as possible to save weight, and thus increase speed. This often leads to gear failures in the course of races, demanding that a member of the crew climb the mast or alternatively be hoisted up it to effect running repairs. This view from a position high up the mast of the Australian yacht *Kookaburra III* emphasizes the height of the mast and size of the sail area currently mounted on the comparatively small hulls of modern racing yachts.

Apart from day racing, the main thrust of yacht racing is devoted to ocean racing. Either between two geographically distant points or alternatively from, and to, the same point via a distant mark. This latter type of racing now includes races across the Atlantic Ocean and several types of round-the-world races. Related to these long-distance races is of course the type of long-distance cruising that appeals to those who can afford the larger and more seaworthy yachts required for ocean cruising.

fast delivery, and these ships became larger than warships, with fine hall lines for speed combined with carrying capacity. Tall masts with huge clouds of sail became common, and larger crews allowed these superb sailing vessels to be sailed to their limits over massive distances. The wool trade with Australia and the tea trade with China were dominated by the great clipper ships until the opening of the Suez Canal in 1869, when the steamship began to rival the clipper on long routes to the eastern hemisphere. The last area in which the great sailing ships still held an edge was South America, where European and American traders needed to round Cape Horn. The sailing ships made the perilous journey more easily than the early steamships, and large four-masted barques and five-masted schooners were the best ships on this route until 1914. In that year, the Panama Canal was opened, and this passage between the Caribbean and the Pacific Ocean removed most of the need for ships to sail around Cape Horn.

World War I ended the day of the sailing ship as the chief trading vessel of the advanced countries: German submarine and surface raiders sank many sailing ships that lacked the speed to escape, and the Allies concentrated their shipbuilding on the steam-driven ships that were already in a dominant position. By the middle of the 1970s, the large sailing ship had disappeared, with the exception of some 35 ships used for sail training. Larger numbers of smaller sailing vessels survive as leisure and training vessels in the more advanced countries, and vast numbers of small sail-powered vessels survive in the Far East and Pacific. In the Far East, they serve a vital function on the rivers of China and in the coastal and inter-island waters of southeast Asia and the 13,000 Indonesian islands. In the Pacific, sailing vessels are still the most important trade and communication link in that vast ocean's island groups.

In the Western world, the most important use of sail today is for recreation and competitive sport, ranging from small dinghies with centerboards instead of keels, through twin-hulled catamarans and three-hulled trimarans used for long-distance cruising and oceanic races, to the 'blue ribbon' offshore racing boats with a length of 75ft and a substantial crew. Undoubtedly, the best-known of the racing sailboats are the 12-meter yachts used in the America's Cup series. Yachting has been popular with the wealthy since the middle of the 17th century, and became increasingly widespread in the 18th and 19th centuries. But it is only in the 20th century that sailboats have become as immensely popular as they are today, catering for every degree of skill, enthusiasm, and wealth.

Steamships

Sailing ships have the great advantage of using a source of power – the wind – that is entirely free. Movement therefore is cheap, because the sailing ship's outfit of masts, spars, and sails is fairly long-lasting. Only a small amount of the hull's volume need be devoted to carrying spare sails and spars, leaving most of the hull free for the carriage of cargo in merchant ships or of men and armament in warships. On the other side of the coin, however, are the facts that sailing ships are tied to prevailing weather conditions and cannot sail directly into the wind. The first of these disadvantages results in slow sailing speed with light winds, and the second requires the ship either to zigzag slowly against the wind (a process known as 'tacking') or to sail off-course in the search of favorable winds: in both cases, the result is a voyage lasting much longer than planned.

In the past, this sometimes meant that the crew's food and water began to run out, but until that happened, the speed generally did not matter too much when the ship involved was a merchantman carrying a non-perishable bulk cargo such as timber, coal, or grain. For warships, though, the difficulties and peculiarities of the wind often meant the difference between victory or defeat.

Mechanical power obviously offers a way around this problem, but it was not available until the second half of the 18th century and the development of the first steam engines. The first practical steam engine was patented by a Briton, James Watt, in 1769, and was suc-

Early steamships burned their coal fuel so extravagantly that it was a sensible precaution and also an economic advantage to carry sails that could replace the steam engine if it broke down or ran out of fuel, or alternatively supplement the effort of the steam engine when the wind was favorable. This early steamship, with its main propulsive effort provided by two paddle wheels, also carries five sails in the form of a jib, two topsails and two drivers.

period. The paddles were mounted on a common shaft driven by the midships-mount engine and generally had six or more blades.

The early steam engines were not very efficient, and their fuel consumption was high. This was not a particular problem for vessels that did not venture far from a coal station, so most of the early steam vessels were therefore harbor and river tugs, gradually extending to coastline vessels that could come into harbor if coal stocks were low. Gradually, the advantages of steam for deep-ocean vessels became clearer, though it was designed to supplement rather than supplant sail: if the wind was in the right quarter and of adequate strength, the sails were used; but if the wind was wrong in strength or direction, the steam engine could be used to maintain progress along the desired course. The tendency was not to use the engine unless absolutely necessary – merchant captains did not want to use expensive coal unless it was unavoidable, and naval captains disliked the damage to their snowy sails and decks caused by the engine's smut and smoke.

Given the emphasis still placed on sail, it was sensible to make the paddle wheels as units that could be dismantled and stowed on deck when not in use. Typical of ships that followed this practice were the American 380-ton steam packet *Savannah*, claimed in 1819 to be the first steam vessel to have crossed the Atlantic. The *Savannah* had been built as a pure sailing vessel, but was later fitted with an auxiliary steam engine and dismountable paddle wheels. In 1819, she made her celebrated crossing of the Atlantic from Savannah to Liverpool in 21 days, but was in fact under power for only 8 hours! The first ship to make a crossing of the North Atlantic entirely on steam power was the *Sirius*, a 700-ton British ship designed for ferry operations across the English Channel and powered by a 320hp steam engine. In 1838, she was chartered by the British and American Steam Navigation Company, which had pinned great commercial hopes on achieving the first steam-powered

Top: The task in which paddlewheelers, such as the *Monarch* illustrated here, survived for the longest time was ferrying, especially in places such a rivers and harbors where the paddlewheeler's great agility could be used to advantage.

Above center: The side boxes of a paddlewheeler gave an ungainly appearance but produced considerable agility useful in craft such as the *Griper*, which operated as a harbor tug.

Above: The *Waverley* is one of the longest-lived paddlewheelers, and is still used for tourist trips on the south coast of England.

Atlantic crossing in a ship built especially for the task. But with its *British Queen* late in delivery and Brunel's *Great Western* still unfinished, the company chartered the *Sirius* and dispatched her from Cork in Ireland on April 4, 1838, with 40 passengers: she arrived in New York 18 days later after crossing at an average of 6.7 knots, beating the *Great Western* by just a few hours, despite the fact that Brunel's ship had left Bristol four days after the departure of the *Sirius* from Cork. After using all her coal, the *Sirius* had been forced to burn all the cabin furniture, the spare spars, and even one mast! Typical of the early hybrids used as warships was the British frigate HMS *Galatea* of 1829.

By about 1840, it was common for the blades of the paddle wheels to be fitted with a feathering device (radial rods operated by an eccentric wheel) to keep the blades as nearly vertical as possible as they entered, moved through, and finally came out of the water: this feature increased the power of the blades in the water and reduced wash, with advantages to speed and fuel economy.

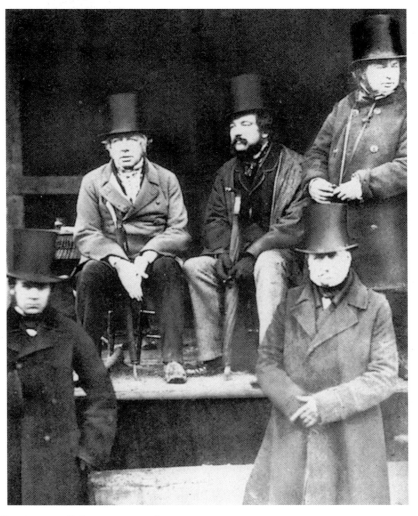

One of the greatest ship designers of his time, and indeed one of the greatest engineers of the period, was Isambard Kingdom Brunel, seen here at the launch of the *Great Eastern*, the third and last of his epoch-making steamships with a displacement of over 18,000 tons when few other large ships had a displacement of more than 5,000 tons.

A major turning point in the development of steamships was the construction of the *Great Western*, which was built of wood. She was 236ft. long and half of her interior volume was occupied by coal, four boilers, and the two-cylinder Maudsley engine that drove the two paddle wheels. On her maiden voyage from Bristol to New York in 1838, carrying 24 first-class passengers, the ship averaged eight knots and achieved the crossing in 15 days. She arrived in New York with 200 tons of coal remaining. The success of the *Great Western* confirmed that purpose-designed steamships were more economical than converted sailing ships or purpose-built hybrid types, and also proved that it was safe to operate long oceanic routes with ships powered entirely by steam.

The result was considerable growth in the number and importance of paddle-wheel steamships. The UK was by far the largest maritime power of the period, and the routes from British ports that saw the greatest growth in steamship traffic were those across the Atlantic, to the Iberian peninsula (northern Spain, Lisbon, and Gibraltar) and into the Mediterranean, and later in the century through the Suez Canal toward India and the Far East. Coaling stations were developed in strategically placed ports and islands, allowing the steady development of steam-powered trade routes to South America, South Africa, and Australasia.

One of the most celebrated, or perhaps notorious, steamships of all time was the *Titanic*, flagship of the White Star line. Displacing 46,300 tons, the ship was generally regarded as unsinkable, but was lost on her maiden voyage in April 1912 after striking an iceberg that tore a great hole in her side. There were 2,201 persons on board, but the lifeboats could carry a maximum of only 1,178 people, so despite the fact that the ship sank only slowly, 1,490 people were lost – 916 passengers (including 106 women and 52 children) and 673 members of the crew. Part of the casualty total is attributable to the fact that many people, believing that the ship was indeed unsinkable, initially refused to board the lifeboats. These were lowered to the water only half filled, and when it finally became clear that the ship was actually sinking, many jumped into the water and died of exposure or drowning before they could be rescued.

Yet the paddle wheel was already entering its last phase as the means of transmitting the steam engine's power to the water. Merchant seamen had been aware all along that the rolling of a ship in any type of seaway placed great strains on the driveshaft, when one wheel was deep in the water and the other perhaps completely out of the water. The fact that a lightly laden vessel had only part of its wheels submerged, while a deeply laden ship had most of its wheels under the water made it difficult to plan the size and storage of an economical load of coal. Naval officers were aware of the paddle wheel's limitations for another reason: even when protected by large paddle boxes, the wheels were very vulnerable to the type of broadside fire that was the mainstay of naval gunnery in this period.

For these reasons, therefore, the emphasis turned slowly but inevitably to the propeller, which remains safely submerged in all but the most extreme circumstances. It should not be imagined that the development of effective propeller drives 'killed off' the paddle wheel at a stroke. Existing ships, built to the exacting standards of strength and reliability common in the last three-quarters of the 19th century, proved too reliable and workmanlike for early scrapping, and therefore remained in service. In passenger ships, there was a certain resistance to propellers, moreover, for passengers appreciated the sense of security provided by the sight of a massive paddle churning the water on each side of the ship. The Cunard Line continued to commission paddle-wheel steamships for its Atlantic routes right up to 1861, ending with the superb *Scotia* powered by Napier engines, which had 100in diameter cylinders with 144in stroke pistons, and generated 4,600hp to give the ship a speed of 16 knots.

As the paddle wheel slowly disappeared from ocean-going ships, it remained important for specialized vessels, chiefly tugs and river or lake craft. One of the great advantages of the paddle wheel over the propeller is the fact that it develops very nearly as much power in reverse as in forward drive. This has particular advantages in a tug, providing for rapid stopping and reversing in the confined waters of a harbor. At the same time, the tug can be fitted with the means to disengage the drive to either paddle, allowing one to drive while the other freewheels, or even goes into reverse, to allow the tug to turn in its own length, a feat impossible with a propeller-driven tug. Such tugs have survived to the present day in a number of forms; some of the most recent have a diesel engine powering an electric generator that supplies current to the motor driving each wheel.

Lake and river operations place great emphasis on flat-bottom and shallow-draft vessels, to reduce the chances of the vessel being grounded in shallow water or on shoals, and in the event of this happening, of suffering the least possible damage. All over the world, paddle wheelers remained in service, and indeed in development, for use on rivers and lakes, long after propeller-driven ships had replaced them for ocean-going purposes. On the lakes of Africa, the Americas, Asia, and Europe, paddle wheelers were a common sight right into this century, and the great rivers of Africa, Asia, and South America were ably served by paddle wheelers, operating on such famous watercourses as the Nile, Ganges, Yangtze, and Amazon. For military operations, there were large numbers of paddle-powered river gunboats that remained in service right up to World War II.

The best known of these paddle wheelers are the classic vessels that plied the waterways of the central United States: the Mississippi, Missouri, and Ohio rivers and, to a lesser extent, the Great Lakes. About half of these paddle wheelers were of the stern-wheel type, with a single wheel mounted at the stern. This wheel extended across virtually the full beam of the vessel and was of the simplest type. It had no feathering blades, but was driven directly by a pair of long-stroke pistons located on the sides of the vessel just forward of the paddle wheel, and fed with steam from boilers located fairly close to the bow to preserve the vessel's balance. All the machinery and accommodation was located above deck, allowing the hull to be built with the shallowest possible draft. About 50 per cent of North American paddle wheelers were of this type, which was also the most common found on the shallow rivers and lakes of Africa, Australia, China, India, and the Near East.

The *Lusitania* of the Cunard line is another very famous steamship for much the same reason as the *Titanic*. Built in 1906 and displacing 31,500 tons, the ship was used on the prestigious North Atlantic run between Liverpool and New York. In 1907 she captured the Atlantic "blue riband" with a crossing at 23.99 kt. The ship continued her Atlantic service after the outbreak of world War I, and despite Germans warnings that she was liable to attack still attracted large numbers of passengers including many Americans. The captain had been ordered to steer a zigzag course and avoid obvious landfalls, but ignored his instructions in May 1915 and arrived off the Old Head of Kinsale in Ireland steering a straight course. Here the virtually unthinkable happened when the German submarine U-20 fired two torpedoes into her. The ship sank in about 20 minutes, and went down by the bows so rapidly that it was impossible to launch some of the lifeboats. This resulted in the loss of 1,198 lives, 124 of them American. This was one of the factors that helped to exacerbate American feelings in February 1917, when Germany declared a policy of unrestricted submarine warfare, and was thus instrumental in the USA's declaration of war on Germany in April 1917.

the ship faster through the water than paddle wheels on the same horsepower, and also that it exerted more power in the water. Fairly rapid development followed this trial. The two-blade propeller with long narrow blades was overtaken by propellers with shorter and wider blades, of which three and then four were carried. The original arrangement of the propeller was as a single unit on the center line of the hull, but to absorb the increased power of later engines, this configuration was steadily modified to two propellers (one on each quarter), three propellers (one centerline and two quarter units) and finally four propellers (two on each quarter).

Though initially sponsored by the Royal Navy, the propeller found its first real acceptance in merchant shipping. Brunel designed the 3,270-ton *Great Britain* as a side-wheeler, but then modified the design for propeller propulsion. In other respects, too, the *Great Britain* marked a new beginning in ship design. Laid down in 1839, launched in 1843, and commissioned in 1845, the ship was 322 ft. long, was the first transatlantic liner built of iron rather than wood, and for safety was divided into six watertight compartments separated by special bulkheads. The ship had six masts, but was designed principally for steam, with her engines delivering 1,500 hp to the propeller by an innovatory chain drive. On her maiden voyage to New York, she carried 60 first-class passengers, a considerably larger number of steerage-class passengers, and 600 tons of cargo. She ran aground at the end of her return crossing, but was refloated 11 months later with minimal damage. Later, she was used for passenger and cargo carrying on the run to Australia. About 40 years after she entered service,

Below and bottom: In the period between the last quarter of the 19th century and the middle of the 20th century, most of the world's trade was carried by relatively small cargo steamships. There was nothing glamorous about these vessels, in which cargo capacity and reliability was far more important than speed. The required reliability was ensured by the use of steam engines which had by this time reached a peak of capability for steady running on a modest consumption of coal for very long periods. Such ships traversed the world's oceans taking manufactured goods from the more industrialized nations to less well developed countries and returning with raw materials and food etc. The design of such ships was fairly standard, with the bridge, accommodation, and engine room in the center of the hull with holds fore and aft of this block. The holds were generally covered with battened tarpaulins, and the cargo was swayed into and out of the holds by steam-powered mast derricks.

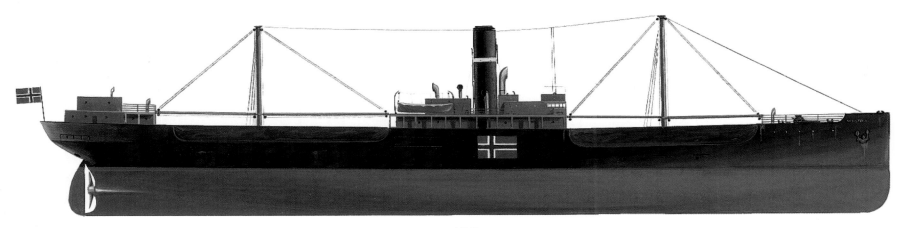

Top and above: While the ships on the preceding page are typical of the smaller cargo ships of the period up to 1940, these two vessels are more typical of the larger general merchantmen that came to the fore in the period between the two world wars. These ships had more refined hull lines with a sharper bow and a greater length/beam ratio, and could supplement the revenues from their basic cargo-carrying role with the fees of a small number of passengers. This dictated the creation of a larger and more comfortable accommodation block, although this was generally located in the middle of the ship with holds fore and aft of it.

the *Great Britain* was beached as a coal hulk at Port Stanley in the Falkland Islands, but was recovered in 1970 and returned to her building dock for reconstruction as a superb monument.

Brunel capitalized on all his experience in the construction of his third great steam masterpiece, the *Great Eastern*. At a time when no other ship in the world displaced more than 5,000 tons, the *Great Eastern* was designed for 18,914 tons as the means of carrying 4,000 passengers (or as a troopship for 10,000 soldiers), plus 6,000 tons of cargo. The ship was intended for the route to India and Australia without recoaling, and 11,000hp were delivered by the separate engines, installed for the two side paddles and one four-blade propeller 24 ft. in diameter. The ship was 692ft long, with a beam of 82ft, and could achieve 15 knots. Brunel introduced a power-operated rudder mechanism, and built-in yet more safety features, most notably a cellular double bottom to minimize damage and flooding if the ship should run aground. Laid down in 1854 and launched in 1858, the *Great Eastern* was too far ahead of her time. She bankrupted her builder, ruined Brunel's health, and was then wrongly used for the transatlantic run rather than the Australasian run. As a result, she was a commercial failure, but later achieved greater success as a tele-

Below: The *Norrix* is typical of the type of small coastal cargo vessel still encountered in most parts of the world. The type emphasizes utility and versatility over all other design factors, and generally had a shallow draft.

LMS EXPRESS & CUNARD LINER
The HIGHEST STANDARD OF COMFORT IN RAIL AND OCEAN TRAVEL

graph cable-layer, placing four transatlantic cables, as well as another between Aden and Bombay. She was beached and broken up in 1888.

The use of iron instead of wood as the main structural material for hulls completely altered the nature of ships using both steam and sail propulsion. The first steamship of iron construction was the *Aaron Manly*, which had a Bell engine and side paddles. She made her first voyage in 1820, carrying passengers from London around the coast of Kent, across the English Channel and up the River Seine to Paris, at an average speed of between eight and nine knots. The ship made this run several times and was then bought by a Parisian group for excursions up and down the Seine from Paris. The ship was extremely important in the science of shipbuilding, and her novel construction rapidly became standard from merchant ships in the 1830s and 1840s. Naval construction lagged, with even steam vessels built largely of wood, but commercial interests were quick to appreciate the advantages of the reliability and low maintenance costs offered by the combination of steam propulsion and an iron hull. As noted above, Brunel pushed forward the concept of iron construction with enormous far-sightedness, and by the 1870s and 1880s, 20,000-ton passenger liners were relatively common as world trade and migration expanded.

Iron was slowly overtaken by steel as the main structural medium, allowing the development of larger and stronger hulls; this development in size was matched by improved engines so that performance did not suffer. All these early steam engines were of the reciprocating type, in which one or more cylinders each contain a piston driven by steam for an up-and-down motion translated into the circular motion of the paddle(s) or propeller(s) by the throw of a crankshaft linked to the piston by a connecting shaft. In the early engines, the steam was supplied from the boiler at low pressure, and, after powering the piston, was expelled from the cylinder into a condenser that turned it back into water, which was then returned to the boiler for re-use.

In 1854, John Elder introduced the compound engine, which had been patented as early as 1781 by Jonathan Hornblower, but then had to wait for 75 years before becoming practical after the development of boilers able to generate enough pressure of steam (about 40lb per square inch). In the compound engine, the steam expelled from the main cylinder is passed through a second, low-pressure cylinder before passing to the condenser: the compound engine's secondary use of the steam adds to the thrust generated on the crankshaft, thereby increasing the efficiency of the engine for a given quantity of steam.

Further development of boilers by the adoption of forced air measures allowed an increase in pressure to about 125lb per square inch, making possible the triple-expansion engine as first installed in the steamer *Propontis* by Dr A C Kirk during 1874. This was a logical development of the compound engine with high-, intermediate- and low-pressure cylinders to wring maximum effort out of the steam before it reached the condenser and became water once more. Limited use was also made of a quadruple-expansion engine, most notably in the German liners built between 1897 and 1902, such as the Kaiser Wilhelm der Grosse.

High-pressure steam was also highly important for the handling of the cargoes carried by merchant ships. It is comparatively simple to pipe steam to a desired spot, where an engine can be located to drive winches; this enabled the use of small and economical crews to load and unload the increasingly large volume of the world's trade carried in steamships right up to World War II.

Enormous development, and indeed success, was achieved by these reciprocating engines, but the limitation of any such engine using a piston is that the up-and-down (linear or straight-line) motion of the piston has to be turned into the revolutionary (rotating) motion of the propeller. The piston has to change direction through 180 degrees at the top and bottom of each stroke, resulting in great strain on the connecting rod, large loss of power, and considerable vibration in the engine; and the translation of power from the linear to the revolutionary mode results in considerable mechanical waste. The solution was the turbine engine, in which the high-pressure steam is introduced to a series of blades set at an angle on a turning drum, which is connected either directly or via gears to the propeller shaft. The steam spins the turbine, which generates relatively vibration-free power in the same axis as the propeller. Developed first by Sir Charles

Opposite, top: A poster advertisement for the LMS railroad and Cunard emphasizes the convenience of long-distance travel for the affluent passengers of the 1930s: the steam train delivered the passenger from his home to the dockside in considerable comfort. The passenger had then merely to board the ship as his luggage was loaded by the companies' employees.

Opposite, below: This is the Cunard line's 81,237-ton *Queen Mary*, which was launched in September 1934 and entered service in June 1936. Together with the slightly larger *Queen Elizabeth*, the *Queen Mary* marked one of the high points in the development of the steamship as a luxury liner, and in 1938 secured the undisputed Atlantic "blue riband" accolade with westbound and eastbound speeds of 30.99 and 31.69 kt respectively. In World War II the ship operated as a troop transport with capacity steadily increased from 8,200 to 15,000 men, and so fast was the ship that she was deemed immune to submarine interception, and allowed to operate outside the escorted convoy system. Between April 1943 and the end of World War II in May 1945, the *Queen Mary* and similarly converted *Queen Elizabeth* carrying 320,000 US troops across the Atlantic to the UK.

Right: The *Queen Elizabeth* had a gross tonnage of 82,998 tons, and was still being outfitted after her launch in September 1938 when World War II started in September 1939. The ship was used as a troop transport in World War II and finally entered commercial service in October 1946.

Parsons in the UK, turbine power was initially demonstrated in Parsons' own *Turbinia* of 1894: this novel 45-ton vessel created an enormous impression when she appeared at Queen Victoria's 1897 Diamond Jubilee Naval Review at Spithead, with her three turbines delivering 2,000shp for a speed of just under 35 knots. This was a quite unprecedented speed at a time when the fastest naval vessels could achieve only 25 knots on their fully developed triple-expansion engines. Turbines were rapidly adopted by the world's navies and by more far-sighted merchant operators, and really came into their own with the adoption of oil-fired boilers in place of the coal-fired ones that had been used up to that time.

The combination of oil-fired boilers and steam turbines transformed steamships more than any other single advance in the previous 75 years, disposing with the laborious and dirty task of coaling the ship at frequent intervals, thus removing the need for a large number of stokers, and boosting the range on a given volume of fuel. The oil-fired boiler/steam turbine combination remained standard until after World War II, when the gas turbine and the diesel engine largely replaced it. The gas turbine offers very high power for very small size and light weight, while the diesel engine offers exceptional reliability and economy. Merchant ships generally rely on diesels alone, and warships frequently combine a diesel for cruising with a gas turbine outfit for combat.

The size of steam-powered liners peaked at about 80,000 tons during the period between the world wars, when they were unquestionably the 'last word' in luxury travel. After World War II, liners found it increasingly difficult to compete with air transport, and the breed has virtually died out with the single exception of the luxury cruise liner with diesel propulsion. Cargo ships have fared somewhat better in the battle with the airplane, but world fleets have shrunk considerably since World War II. With the exception of obsolete types, nearly all today's working cargo ships are diesel-powered.

One of the most luxurious ships currently in service is the Cunard line's *Queen Elizabeth II* which, unlike her predecessor, is a cruise liner rather than a transatlantic passenger liner as the scheduled trans Atlantic crossing market is now dominated by airliners.

Submarines

So far we have restricted ourselves to vessels that move on the surface of the water, and now it is time to consider the type that moves below the surface. This is the submarine, which is a vessel designed and built to operate under the surface of the sea, so that it can avoid the easy detection and destruction that can befall surface vessels. The ability to 'sneak up' on the enemy has long been a desire of armed forces, and the notion of a submarine vessel therefore had great attraction from early times. There were almost certainly designs (if not prototypes) in the period up to the end of the 16th century, but no known records of these efforts survive.

In the years between 1575 and 1865 many submarines were designed, and the designs of at least 17 survive today. The four men who made the greatest strides in this difficult field were the Englishman William Bourne, the Dutchman Cornelius van Drebbel, and the Americans David Bushnell and Robert Fulton. It was the two Americans who made the most notable contributions.

Bushnell was born in 1742 and graduated from Yale in 1775, just before the beginning of the War of Independence. Bushnell was bitter in his opposition to the British, and designed a small 'submarine.' This Turtle was shaped like an egg, and by the flooding of two small internal tanks it could be trimmed right down in the water so that its conning tower was awash. Propulsion was provided by a hand-cranked propeller, and offensive capability rested with a 150lb charge of gunpowder that was designed to be attached to the underside of the

One of the earliest attempts of at least a marginally realistic nature in man's attempt to create a submarine warship was this 1653 catamaran submersible boat built in Amsterdam by a Frenchman, de Son. This boat has the distinction of having been the first mechanically powered submarine ever built, but the wind-up motor proved too weak to turn the paddlewheel located centrally between the two hulls.

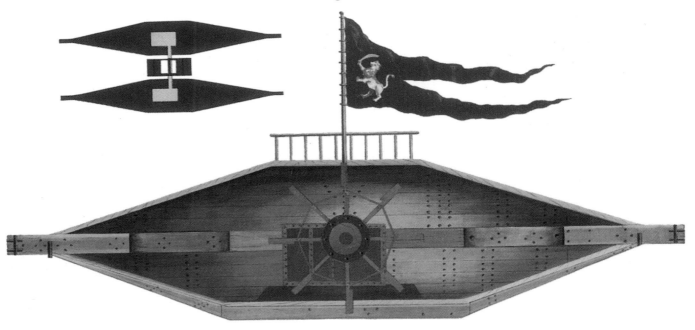

target ship by a screw. In 1776, the Bushnell 'submarine' was launched against the British fleet lying off New York: manned by Sergeant Ezra Lee, the 'submarine' reached the Eagle, flagship of Admiral Lord Howe, but could not deposit its charge, as Bushnell had forgotten that British warships were plated with copper, which resisted the penetration of the screw. Two other unsuccessful efforts were made later in the war, but in 1782, Bushnell gave up his efforts and became a doctor.

Fulton was born in 1765, and after an early working life as a jeweler's apprentice and portrait painter, he decided that engineering should be his career. In 1794, he traveled to England and became involved in canal engineering, but, in 1797, he moved to France and attempted to persuade the French that they needed submarines to defeat the British at sea. In 1801, Fulton managed to persuade Napoleon of his concept's validity, and received 10,000 francs to design and build a prototype, the Nautilus. The submarine was ellipsoid in shape, 21ft long, and 7ft in maximum diameter. It could be submerged by opening cocks to flood internal tanks. Surface propulsion was provided by a (collapsible) mast and sail, and underwater propulsion by hand-cranked propeller. A first test in Brest was successful when the Nautilus placed an external charge under a schooner anchored in the harbor, but the French marine ministry remained skeptical. Fulton tried his luck in Britain, but with equal lack of success, and then returned to the USA, where his concept was also turned down. In 1812, Fulton devised his 'turtle-boat,' a semi-submersible for operations against the British in the War of 1812: this boat was propelled by a hand-cranked propeller and designed to flood down to a freeboard of only 6in, so that the craft could, at night, be mistaken for a floating log. The 'weapon' carried by the turtle-boat was a series of towed floating charges which could be swung against the target vessel and detonated from a safe distance with a lanyard. The first trial was not successful, and the turtle-boat was then destroyed by a British raiding party before its trials could be continued. Fulton went on to make his name as a pioneer of steam power for ships.

The semi-submersible was also used in the Civil War (1861-

1865). The type used by the Confederate navy carried the name 'David.' The 'Davids' were intended to redress the considerable numerical superiority of the Union navy and came in two basic forms, using steam or hand power. The best-known exploit of a steam-powered 'David' was the attack on the Federal ship New Ironsides in Charleston harbor in October, 1863: under the command of Lieutenant Glassel, the 'David' did not get close enough to the ship before its spar torpedo (a 75lb explosive charge at the end of a long pole) was exploded, and the resulting waves swamped and sank the semi-submersible. More success attended a hand-propelled 'David,' the H.L. Hunley, committed against the Federal ship Housatonic just as she was about to get under way in February, 1864: the Housatonic was holed and opened to the sea. She sank, taking down with her the successful 'David,' whose crew of nine was found inside the sunken vessel when divers went down to the wrecks some years later.

Clearly, a successful submarine depends on a number of primary requirements: a hull of circular section to withstand water pressure when submerged; ballast tanks that can be filled with water to make the submarine sink, and then refilled with air to restore the buoyancy and bring it back to the surface; a powerplant able to function without a constantly replenished supply of air when the submarine is submerged; a rudder to provide directional control; and horizontal rudders (hydroplanes) to provide longitudinal control. The hydroplanes also need to be controllable either collectively so that, for example, a positive angle on both planes will bring the submarine upward without changing its lon-

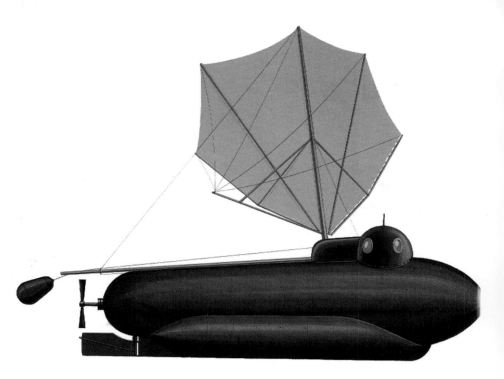

Opposite: These are two views of the Bushnell *Turtle* with its hand-cranked propeller at the front for tractive power, and its rudder and floating 'bomb' at the rear. The vertically mounted hand-cranked propeller was used for vertical movement, and just to its rear is the similarly hand-operated screw to attach the bomb to the hull of the target vessel.

Top: Robert Fulton's *Nautilus* had a sail to ease the task of the crew, who had otherwise to turn the propeller with a hand crank, and carried its explosive charge at the end of a trailing wire.

Above: Wilhelm Bauer's iron *Plongeur Marin* of 1850 had a central wheel to move the fore-and-aft movement of the weight that controlled the 'submarine' in a series of dips.

Below: The CSS *H.L. Hunley* was a submersible of the Confederate navy in the American Civil War, and was propeled by a propeller cranked by eight men. This was the first submarine to sink a ship, an event that occurred in February 1864 when the spar torpedo was driven into the side of the USS *Housatonic*, a Federal sloop blockading Charleston, South Carolina.

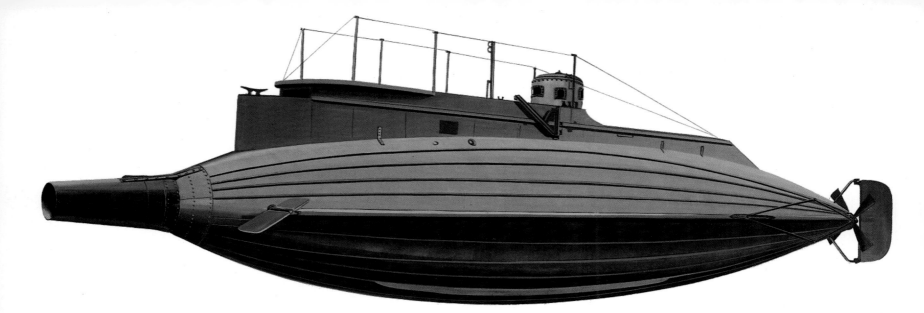

gitudinal angle, or differentially for a bow-up or bow-down angle to speed surfacing or submerging.

The development of metal construction for ships opened the possibility of a watertight hull of considerable strength without excessive thickness and, during the second half of the 19th century, American and French inventors developed a number of designs up to model form. None of them secured the official backing that could have turned them into full-size hardware. This was perhaps just as well, for the major problems yet to be overcome were underwater propulsion and an effective underwater weapon. Steam power could be used for surface propulsion, of course, but was impractical because of the time needed both to damp down the boilers before submerging and to get up a head of steam after surfacing. The practical solution for surface propulsion appeared in 1885 with the invention of the internal-combustion engine by Gottlieb Daimler: some years had to elapse before it had been made powerful and reliable enough to use on board ships, but it offered the possibility of instant shut-down and start-up. However, such an engine cannot be used under water, since it needs a supply of air so large that the engine would exhaust the submarine's supply of compressed breathing and ballast-blowing air in a very short time.

For underwater running, a combination of electric engines and a massive array of batteries provided one solution, but it had its limitations. Surface running could be entrusted to the internal-combustion engine, which could also be used to charge the batteries of the under-

The Nordenfeldt submarine was a German prototype of 1890, and although little concrete information about the type is available, it appears that the 'snout' at the bow was a torpedo tube.

John Holland's first submarine was the *Plunger*, whose construction was halted because of disagreements between the designer and the US Navy.

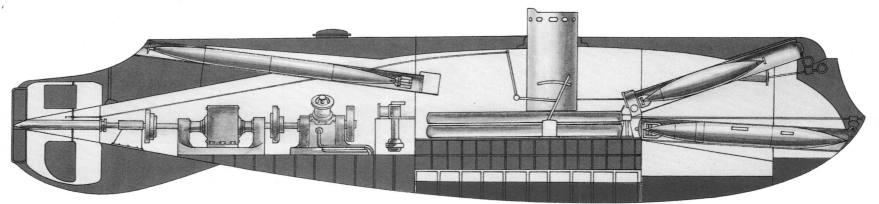

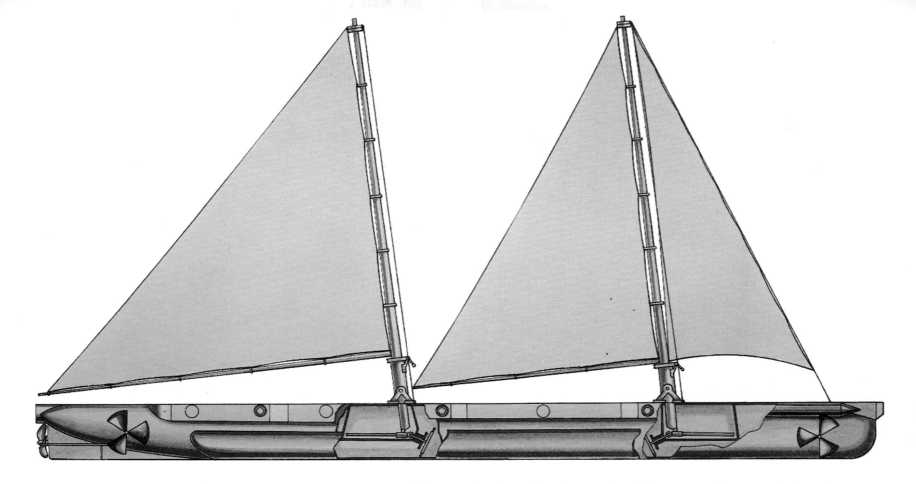

The *Beaver* is typical of early experimental submarines, and was fitted with sails on two hinged masts (the fore and main masts folded down toward the stern and bow respectively) in an attempt to extend the cruising range. The whole concept of masts and sails was impractical for a submarine.

The *Lake Protector* was designed with retractable wheels that could be lowered so that the boat could run along the sea bottom, assuming that this surface was hard or level enough for this purpose. The boat was also designed to halt on the bottom to let out and recover underwater demolition teams.

water system. The main drawback to the idea was the need for the submarine to surface periodically to recharge the batteries, but this problem could be reduced by surfacing at night or in safe conditions. But, the submarine with combined internal-combustion/electrical propulsion should perhaps be thought of as a submersible rather than as a true submarine.

An effective weapon was found in the locomotive torpedo, a free-running weapon developed by Robert Whitehead, a British engineer working at Fiume in Austria-Hungary. The torpedo used compressed air for motive power and had a hydrostatic valve (later a pendulum system) for stability of depth. The first trials were undertaken in 1867, and by 1869 the locomotive torpedo was a practical weapon that was rapidly adopted by most of the world's more advanced navies. The type was still limited, but progress was made steadily in improving the torpedo's range, speed, and course-keeping, the last with the aid of a gyroscopic system invented in Trieste by L Obry in 1881. The first production torpedo emerged from the Royal Laboratory at Woolwich, England, in

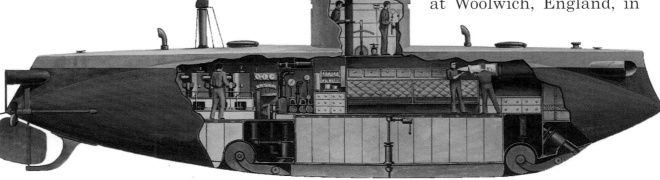

The US Navy's first submarines were Holland-designed 'Plungers' with a cigar-shaped hull and a low casing/conning tower combination.

the early 1870s: it was a 16in weapon with contra-rotating propellers for a range of 1,000 yards at 7 knots or 300 yards at 12.5 knots. The pace of development is indicated by the fact that, in 1909, the standard Whitehead torpedo was an 18in weapon with a range of 2,000 yards at 35 knots or 4,000 yards at 29 knots. Further development was followed through the enrichment of the torpedo's air oxidant: the British developed a steam/gas engine in which water was evaporated and superheated by a shale-oil jet, while the Americans produced the Bliss-Leavitt type with a turbine driven by steam heated by an alcohol torch. By 1914, torpedoes were generally of 18in or 21in diameter, with lengths of 17.5ft and 22ft respectively and with ranges of 3,750 yards at 44 knots or 10,000 yards at 28 knots.

The torpedo was the ideal weapon for the submarine: it was designed to run underwater in any case, and in submarines it could be fired by compressed air out of tubes that could then be reloaded from inside the submarine, if it was large enough to carry a reserve supply.

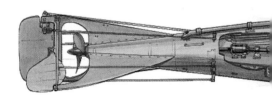

These features all combined in the fertile mind of an Irish-born American, John P Holland, who may be regarded as the father of the true submarine. The first Holland submarine was the Plunger, a design commissioned by the US Navy and built by the Columbian Iron Works in 1896. Because of the naval requirements, the design was too complex for its small size, and the Plunger was not successful. The contract was cancelled in 1900, the year in which the US Navy bought the sole example of Holland's next design, which had been planned as a private venture and built by Crescent. This seven-man vessel had surfaced and submerged displacements of 64 and 74 tons on a length of 53.75ft, and with 50hp available from its gasoline or electric engines, had surfaced and submerged speeds of 8 and 5 knots respectively.

In the mid-1930s the Japanese navy began experiments with small two-man midget submarines which, it felt, could penetrate into enemy harbors and other target areas inaccessible to larger boats. Two prototypes were followed by 41 examples of the 'Type A' class. With electric propulsion the boats were designed to be released close to their targets by modified seaplane carriers. The boats were notably unsuccessful in their first operations, and the survivors were relegated to the defense of major Japanese bases.

The armament included one 18in torpedo tube and one 8in dynamite gun. The concept clearly held promise, and there followed a group of seven 'A' class submarines which were slightly larger and provided improved underwater performance.

Several other countries began to develop submarines around the turn of the century. Germany was an exception, as its navy preferred to wait for the perfection of the considerably safer and more economical compression (rather than spark) ignition engine, which used diesel oil instead of volatile gasoline. The first Unterseeboot appeared in 1906 as a 19-man vessel that was 139ft long. At surfaced and underwater displacements of 238 and 283 tons, it was capable of 10.7 and 7 knots on its diesel or electric motors, each developing 400hp. The armament was still limited, comprising of just one 17.7in torpedo tube.

Technical progress in the years before World War I was rapid, and by the beginning of the war, there were about 400 submarines in ser-

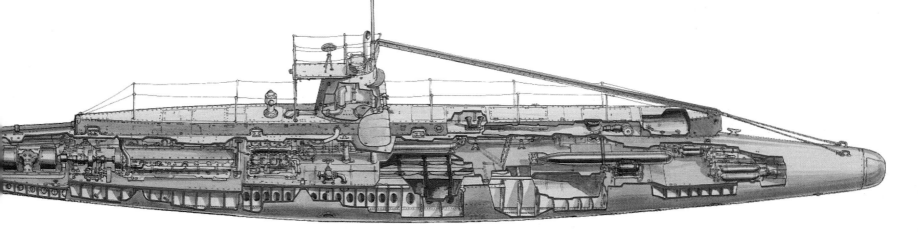

vice with 16 navies. The British and French mustered about half of this total, but whereas these vessels were generally of the small coastal type with a displacement of about 300 tons, the Germans used the larger type suitable for open-sea operations, on a displacement between 550 and 850 tons. The Royal Navy had 71 operational submarines with another 31 being built, and the Germans had 33 with another 28 in production. The British and most other navies saw their submarines as companions to their large surface fleets, to search out and ambush the enemy's warships, but the Germans rapidly came to the conclusion that the submarine could, and should, be used as a deep-sea raider independent of the surface forces.

The Germans led the submarine race right through World War I, building about 450 submarines before the end of the conflict. The maximum number known to have been at sea at any one time is 61, in June 1917, and during the early months of 1917, the Germans' policy of submarine warfare against Allied merchant shipping nearly brought the British and French war efforts to a standstill. More important, however, the unrestricted nature of this campaign

This is a cutaway of the B 11, the last unit of the British 'B' class of coastal submarines, completed in 1915 and 1916 by Vickers. The boat was 135 ft 0 in long, and had surfaced and submerged displacements of 280 and 313 tons respectively. Surfaced propulsion was a 600-hp gasoline engine for a speed of 13 kt, reduced to 9 kt when submerged on the power of the 190-hp electric motor. The armament comprised two 18-in torpedo tubes, and extremely spartan accommodation was provided for the crew of 16.

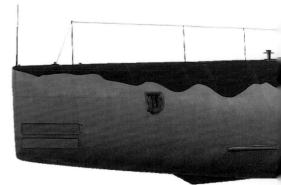

The British 'X' class midget submarine was planned in World War II for specialist tasks such as attacks on moored warships that could not be tackled by motor torpedo boats or bombers. Six austerely equipped training boats, and 12 more fully equipped operational boats were built between 1942, and 1944, and the basic data for these boats included a length 51 ft 3 in, surfaced and submerged displacement of 27 and 30 tons respectively, surface propulsion by a 42-hp diesel engine for a speed of 6.5 kt reducing to 5.5 kt submerged on the power of the 30-hp electric motor, an armament of two 2-ton explosive side charges that were designed to be dropped on the seabed under the target, and a crew of four.

involved attacks on neutral merchantmen, and the sinking of several American ships brought the USA into the war against the Germany. The diversity of Germany's submarine classes shows the various roles that could be undertaken by this important new weapon. For coastal operations, there were the UB and UC types: the UB submarines were designed for gun and torpedo attack on enemy shipping in coastal waters, and displaced between 128 and 550 tons, while the UC submarines were planned as minelayers, and displaced between 170 and 510 tons. For deep-sea operations, there were the Mittel-U types, which displaced between 560 and 900 tons; and ocean-going submarines were also developed in specialized variants, such as the long-range minelayer (UE type of between 750 and 1,160 tons) and the long-range cruiser (UA type of between 1,500 and 3,200 tons) for attacks on enemy shipping in distant waters. Germany also produced a small number of merchantman submarines, known as Handels Unterseeboote, which were designed to ferry vitally needed supplies back to Germany, and was planning other types as the war ended. By the end of the war, German submarines had reached a high level of efficiency, given their basic design features. Most of the submarines could dive to a depth of 280ft, and the larger boats could run submerged for 100 miles at 3 knots or 20 miles at 8 knots. Typical of the late-war Mittel-U type, the 'U99' class submarines carried an armament of four 19.7in torpedo tubes (two bow and two stern), plus one 4.1in gun for more economical strikes on merchant ships when the submarine had surfaced.

Other countries followed basically the same pattern, though only after the Germans' pioneering efforts. Two distinct oddities, however, were the British 'K' and 'M' classes. The 'K' class was designed for high-speed scouting in support of the battle fleet, and at 2,565 tons, it could reach 25 knots on the surface. But, this speed was provided by geared steam turbines delivering 10,500hp! The diving performance

Right: The British response to the Germans' long-range cruising submarines, intended specifically for attacks on shipping in all corners of the world, was the extraordinary 'M' class, of which three were completed (two in 1918 and one in 1920). These boats were 305 ft long and had surfaced and submerged displacement of 1,600 and 1,950 tons respectively. The propulsion arrangement was of the standard diesel/electric arrangement, with the 2,400-hp diesel component providing a surfaced speed of 15.5 kt and the electric arrangement allowing a dived speed of 9.5 kt. The crew was up to 70 men, and the basic torpedo armament was four 18-in tubes in the bow. The most remarkable thing about the 'M' class, however, was the fact that it carried a turreted 12-in gun ahead of the conning tower, designed to provide the boat with the ability to tackle and sink ships at very long range. Only a very limited degree of traverse was possible, for firing over the beam might have capsized the boat. The boats were very clumsy, and the full range of the main gun (supplemented by a 3-in anti-aircraft gun) could not be used as accurate long-range rangefinding was impossible.

of these submarines was very poor, for they needed at least 30 minutes before the submarine could submerge. The 'M' class was planned to provide a 'submarine monitor' capability, and the three submarines of the class each displaced 1,950 tons and possessed, in addition to four 18in torpedo tubes, one 12in gun in a massive installation just forward of the conning tower. The idea was wholly impractical.

During the inter-war years, there was little technical innovation in the design of submarines. The world's major navies concentrated instead on improving the basic concepts proved by the end of World War I. Developments in manufacture, battery design, diesel propulsion, and other features allowed the creation of submarines with better defensive and offensive capabilities, combined with higher performance both on the surface and under water. Larger submarines were built to allow the carriage of more torpedoes and fuel for longer-range operations, and the greater size of the submarines was combined with more carefully considered design to improved 'habitability.' This proved to be an important feature of successful submarine operations: the greater ranges and longer cruises made possible by improved submarines could be used effectively only by crews whose mental and physical health was supported by a more comfortable working environment.

New features were restricted largely to experiments. The most important was perhaps the use of a small airplane for scouting purposes. The British and French made some strides in the development of the concept, using folding seaplanes that could be stowed in a small cylindrical hangar, but the only country to adopt the notion fully was Japan, whose geographical location and anticipated enemies dictated the development of huge submarine raiders carrying seaplanes to scout beyond any submarine's visual horizon. The notion of such scout airplanes became outmoded in World War II with the development of radar, that could fulfill the same role.

Submarine operations in World War II followed the same basic pattern as those of World War I, but were more intense and were undertaken on a global basis. Germany tried to cripple the Allied shipping that kept the UK supplied with food, raw materials, and weapons. From May 1943, however, the German submarine fleet was steadily worn down by the Allies' growing fleets of surface escorts and

One of the most remarkable but also most poorly conceived submarine designs ever was that for the British 'K' class. This was planned to provide high-speed scouting capability for the Grand Fleet in World War I, and was therefore schemed as a type of submersible destroyer with considerable size and a steam powerplant for high surfaced speed. The design, seen here in its original form before the bow was revised into a more bulbous shape, had a length of 338 ft with surfaced and submerged displacements of 1,883 and 2,565 tons respectively. The steam powerplant delivered 10,500 hp to two propellers for a surfaced speed of 25 kt, and the electric motors delivered 1,400 hp for a submerged speed of 9 kt; there was also a diesel engine that could provide 800 hp to boost the diving or surfacing speed. In concept this propulsion arrangement seemed excellent, but if the boat was surprised on the surface, it took at least 20 minutes to damp down the boiler fires, fold the funnels and ensure that all openings had been closed before the boat could dive.

The USS *Torsk* was a boat of the 'Tench' class, one of the most important submarine types built for the US Navy in the later stages of World War II. The type had a length of 311ft 9in with surfaced and submerged displacements of 1,570 and 2,414 tons respectively, and its diesel/electric propulsion arrangement provided 5,400 hp to two shafts for a surfaced speed of 20.25 kts. The primary armaments comprised 24 torpedoes launched through ten 2in tubes (six forward and four aft), and the boat also possessed a three-gun armament of 5-in, 40-mm, and 20-mm weapons. The crew was 90 men, and the boat could dive to 400ft.

airplanes. Using radio direction-finding and radar to detect the German submarines, Allied vessels attacked them after their positions had been fixed by a sound system known to the British as ASDIC (Allied Submarine Detection Investigation Committee), and to the Americans as SONAR (Sound Navigation And Ranging). Airplanes operating from land bases, and from small escort, or 'jeep,' aircraft-carriers, proved decisive in keeping the submarines at bay. As the war progressed, more airplanes were fitted with the radar that allowed them to detect German submarines by day and night in all weathers, severely restricting the freedom of action of the U-boats. Guns for use in the sinking of merchantmen had generally disappeared, but the U-boats were fitted with increasingly powerful batteries of anti-aircraft guns to tackle the Allied airplanes.

The threat of the airplane led to development of the Schnorchel (snorkel), one of the few important technical developments of World War II. This was an air-breathing mast that could be extended, like a periscope, to allow the diesel engines to be run for propulsion and battery-charging while the submarine remained under the surface. The other major German development was the use of a hydrogen peroxide/diesel oil fuel mix for special Walter turbines that generated the power for underwater speeds as fast as 24 knots. Speed of this order was increasingly important as a means of closing in for an attack, and then for evading counterattack by Allied escorts. An effort was made to produce such speeds using conventional electric motors, but while the combination of an extremely streamlined hull with trebled battery capacity did result in 20-knot speeds, such swiftness could be main-

UB-59 was one of the very large 'UB III' class of German submarines in World War I, it had a length of 182 ft, a surfaced displacement of between 508 and 520 tons, a submerged displacement of between 639 and 650 tons, a diesel/electric propulsion arrangement with a 1,100-hp diesel arrangement for a surfaced speed of 13.5 kt and a 788-hp electric arrangement for a submerged speed of 7.5 kt, a crew of 34, and an armament of five 19.7-in torpedo tubes (four bow and one stern) supplemented by one 105-mm or 88-mm gun. The UB-59 was blown up by the Germans as they evacuated their base at Zeebrugge in 1918, but the success of the class at both technical and operational level was directly responsible for the classic 'Type VII' class design of World War II.

tained only for short bursts. The Walter turbines offered higher speed and greater range, but the hydrogen peroxide fuel was dangerous to handle and store, and the system had not been perfected by the end of the war. Some countries tried to take up where the Germans left off, but the Walter turbine concept proved too dangerous for widespread acceptance.

The worsening position in which both Germany and Japan found themselves in 1944 prompted the development of 'odd-ball' submarines, such as midgets, and even human torpedoes, but they fell outside the mainstream of submarine development and remained little more than emergency measures.

The main British submarine effort was made in the Mediterranean, where submarines proved highly successful in cutting the sea routes through which Germany's and Italy's armies in North Africa were supplied from southern France and Italy. The same concept was pursued by the US Navy in the Pacific, where submarines of the large 'Balao,' 'Gato' and 'Tench' classes proved devastating. The submarines of the US Pacific Fleet sank some four million tons of Japanese merchant shipping and a large number of warships, with a loss of only 42 of their own number in combat, with another 18 falling victim to miscellaneous non-combat causes. The warship casualties were a blow to Japan, but the merchant ship losses were devastating. Japan was effectively cut off from its sources of raw materials including oil, and Japan's overseas forces were deprived of weapons, replacements, and reinforcements. Typical of the US submarines that dominated the Pacific War was

HMS *Alaric* of the British 'A' class, which was designed late in world War II with a very long range for operations in the Pacific, and built only in modest numbers before the rest of the boats were canceled. The design had a length of 281 ft 9 in with surfaced and submerged displacements of 1,120 and 1.620 tons respectively, and the diesel/electric propulsion arrangement provided 4,300 hp of diesel power for a surfaced speed of 18 kt and 1,250 hp of electric power for a submerged speed of 18 kt. The primary armament comprised 18-in torpedoes fired by 10 tubes (four internal and two external in the bow complemented by two internal and two external in the stern), and there were also one 3-in gun and one 20-mm cannon. The crew was 60 men. The boat is seen here in its final form with a lengthened hull, a rebuilt bow for better surfaced running, bow sonar, a general improvement in the streamlining of the hull and conning tower, and modernized torpedo tubes.

the 'Tench' class design: it had a crew of 90 men and, at a length of 311.75ft, displaced a maximum of 2,425 tons for a surface speed of 20.25 knots and an underwater speed of 8.75 knots. The armament was ten 21in torpedo tubes (six forward and four aft) with 24 torpedoes and a basic gun fit of one 5in, one 40mm, one or two 20mm, and two 0.5in weapons.

After World War II, the technical expertise of the Germans was closely examined by the Allies, and a number of existing submarines were revised under the US 'Guppy' (Greater underwater propulsive efficiency) project to incorporate the streamlining developed by the Germans late in the war. New submarines were generally built with such streamlining.

Much more important, however, was the development of a totally new type of powerplant, which finally produced a true submarine rather than a submersible. This was the nuclear powerplant, initially developed by Westinghouse under a 1948 contract to the U.S. Atomic Energy Commission. Progress on this powerplant was rapid, and in June 1952, the keel was laid for the world's first nuclear-powered submarine, the USS Nautilus. The nuclear reactor of such a powerplant is used to heat water into steam that then powers a turbine before being condensed back into water for re-use in a closed-cycle system. The turbine generates electricity for the propulsion motors, and the electricity is also used for all submarine functions, including an air purification system. The nuclear-powered submarine is therefore independent of the surface, and the limits to its underwater patrols are now crew endurance and food supplies, which are measured in months, rather than the limitations of the air supply that are envisaged in hours. The nuclear powerplant is large and needs extensive shielding to prevent radiation damage to the crew, but among its many advantages is an undiminishing power output that permits the submarine to maintain its maximum speed virtually indefinitely.

This is USS *Tarpon*, a nuclear-powered attack submarine of the important 'Sturgeon' class delivered between the mid-1960s and mid-1970s. The design has a length of 292 ft 3 in with surfaced and submerged displacements of 4,460 and 4,780 tons respectively, and the 15,000 hp delivered to a single propeller by the nuclear powerplant provides maximum surfaced and submerged speeds in excess of 20 and 30 kt respectively. The boat can dive to a maximum of 1,975 ft, and its primary armament is 23 Mk 48 wire-guided torpedoes launched through four 21-in tubes located amidships and also able to launch UUM-44 SUBROC anti-submarine and/or BGM-109 Tomahawk cruise missiles. The crew is 129 men.

Higher maximum speeds were also made possible by the adoption of a teardrop hull shape in place of the earlier cigar shape: this makes possible an increase in underwater speeds from 25 to 40 knots or more, depending on the submarine's power. As the submarine submerges on leaving harbor, surfacing only at the end of a patrol of perhaps three months, detection is considerably more difficult, especially as the use of new steels for hull construction has allowed a very great increase in maximum diving depth. The conventional diesel/electric submarine of World War II could dive to about 400ft, but modern submarines can descend without difficulty to more than 1,500ft.

The immediate application of nuclear powerplants was to produce nuclear-powered attack submarines armed with torpedoes, by improving on the type of ocean U-boat used by the Germans in World War II. These torpedoes have been radically improved since World War II in terms of speed, range and warhead lethality, but this tendency has in recent years been taken a step further by the adoption of wire guidance. This means that the torpedo trails a thin wire as it leaves its launch tube, allowing the parent submarine's fire-control systems to direct the torpedo right up to target impact. These fire-control systems use advanced computers and the latest sonar sensors to produce a high quality solution to the problem of working out the relative positions of the attacker and target. The heavyweight torpedoes also carry small computer fire-control systems of their own in case a guidance wire breaks, and they can undertake a search and attack on their own. For longer-range attack, there are weapons such as the Subroc (Submarine rocket), launched from a torpedo tube to deliver a homing torpedo to the area in which a target has been detected.

Nuclear power also opened the way for larger submarines carry-

The USS *Barbel* was one of the last diesel/electric-powered submarines delivered to the US Navy, but was notable for the refined nature of the teardrop-shaped hull that was adopted for nuclear-powered boats.

ing ballistic missiles for use in the strategic role. Ground-based missiles launched from silos can be attacked with great accuracy, and air-launched weapons carried by bombers/missile carriers can be destroyed if the launcher is successfully attacked, but the missile-carrying submarine is immensely difficult to detect and attack. The USA and USSR led the way in the development and deployment of such submarines, and the only other countries to have achieved the same capability are the UK, France, and China, which were also the world's only other operators of nuclear-powered attack submarines up to 1995.

The teardrop-shaped hull is more readily discernible in this photograph of the launch of the USS *Dallas*, a member of the 'Los Angeles' class of nuclear-powered attack submarines that forms the main strength of the US Navy's anti-submarine capability in the middle of the 1990s. The design has a length of 360 ft with a submerged displacement of 6,950 tons, and the 35,000 hp delivered to a single propeller by the twinned nuclear powerplant provides maximum surfaced and submerged speeds of 18 and 31kt respectively. The boat can dive to a maximum of 2,460 ft, and its primary armament is 26 Mk 48 wire-guided torpedoes launched through four 21-in tubes located amidships and also able to fire UGM-84 anti-ship missiles and BGM-109 Tomahawk cruise missiles. The crew is 133 men.

Navigation on long underwater patrols would be nearly impossible without today's extraordinarily accurate inertial navigation systems, which after several months, are only a few yards out in their calculations. This accuracy of navigation is essential for launching ballistic missiles, for unless the missile knows exactly where it is at the moment of launch, it cannot arrive accurately on its target. The first US submarine-launched missiles were heavy-weight cruise missiles such as the Regulus, but far more capable are the ballistic missiles, whose three main families have been the Polaris, Poseidon and Trident, that have introduced successive major improvements in terms of payload, range and accuracy. The same is true of the larger number of Soviet missile types produced in parallel with the American weapons. The world's largest submarines are designed to carry and launch nuclear-armed ballistic missiles: the US Navy's 'Ohio' class submarine has a dived displacement of 18,750 tons and carries 24 Trident missiles, while the still more massive 'Typhoon' class submarine of the Soviet (now Russian) Navy has a dived displacement of about 30,000 tons and carries 20 SS-N-20 missiles.

These monsters will remain in service for years to come, but will be improved as more modern missiles become available. Most important, however, are greater speed and reduced noise, and here the British have led the way with the adoption of pump-jet rather than propeller propulsion. Other classified features such as sound-absorbent coatings have also been introduced, and the Russians have pioneered the use of titanium rather than steel in the hull of their 'Alfa' class attack submarines to increase the diving depth to 3,280ft or more. More compact, yet more powerful, nuclear reactors have also raised maximum submerged speeds to well over 40 knots.

Some countries cannot afford nuclear-powered submarines, and in such instances the diesel/electric attack submarine is still very much in use. Recent designs have been notable for their good speed and useful dived range, but the most important feature of modern diesel/electric submarines is their virtually silent operation, which gives them a potential advantage over nuclear-powered attack submarines in shallow waters. Significant strides are being made in the metallurgical, hydrodynamic, electronic, high-capacity battery and related fields, so the development of the submarine is still very much a 'live' subject.

The ultimate word in Western deterrent capability is provided by the vast 'Ohio' class submarines, each carrying 24 Trident nuclear-tipped ballistic missiles. The design has a length of 560 ft with surfaced and submerged displacements of 16,600 and 18,700 tons respectively, and the 60,000 hp delivered to a single propeller by the twinned nuclear powerplant provides maximum surfaced and submerged speeds of 28 and 30 kt respectively. The boat can dive to a maximum of 1,640 ft, and its other armament is Mk 48 wire-guided torpedoes launched through four 21-in tubes located in the bow. The crew is 155 men.

Air Transportation

Airliners

In the modern world, airliners are such an everyday feature of life that it is often forgotten that air transport has existed for little more than three-quarters of a century, and true airline travel for only about 70 years. Yet the origins of the idea are somewhat older, for the aircraft pioneers of the 19th century, especially those in Victorian England, believed firmly in air transport as a means of linking the far-flung corners of the world, but their ambitious schemes were hampered by the fact that, in a period in which no powered heavier-than-air craft had yet flown, they wanted in typical Victorian fashion to start not just with simple machines that could carry a few people over a short distance but rather with enormous, and thus completely impractical, steam-powered machines able to carry sizable passenger loads over considerable ranges.

Even after the Wright brothers started the true era of heavier-than-air flight in 1903, it was many years before the airplane had reached

Seen here while being refueled, the Ford Model 5-AT tri-motor transport was a classic design of its period, and offered the very real benefit of metal-built durability to its more obvious advantages of reliability, and the safety, that came from the use of a powerplant of three air-cooled radial piston engines.

the stage at which it could carry a useful load with anything approaching reliability. Great efforts were made to pioneer passenger transport, air mail, and even rudimentary freight transport in heavier-than-air craft, but the first real success was achieved by the Germans with their lighter-than-air Zeppelin airships. A semi-scheduled service between Hamburg and other German cities

in the period 1901-14 was operated with a small fleet of five airships, such as the LZ-10 Schwaben and LZ-11 Viktoria Luise. About 35,000 passengers were carried without undue incident. However, the greatest strides toward heavier-than-air transport were made in Russia, where Igor Sikorsky's Bolshoi was the world's first four-engined airplane, in this instance a large biplane airliner powered by four 100hp engines. The speed of this pioneering 'airliner' was low, as might be imagined from the combination of a simple and very 'draggy' airframe with very low-powered engines, and this fascinating airplane even possessed a drafty open promenade deck on top of the fuselage!

The world's first scheduled air services were flown in the USA, where the Benoist airline used a trim little seaplane of its own design to carry 1,200 passengers across the bay between Tampa and St. Petersburg, Florida, in the period between January and May 1914. But the slow progress toward viable airlines, made possible by the increased reliability, safety and payload-carrying capability of the airplanes of the time, was suddenly and rudely halted in 1914 when the European nations became involved in World War I. This grim war totally stopped the development of commercial flight, but in the longer term provided the impetus in four years for the development of very much more capable airplanes. The demands of the war in general, and the desire to bomb the enemy in particular, led to faster and sturdier airplanes able to carry large loads with regularity on increasingly reliable and powerful engines. In four years of war, far greater progress was made than in the previous 11 years of powered flight.

The first aeroplane produced by the Douglas Aircraft Company, now part of the great McDonnell Douglas conglomerate, the Cloudster was designed in 1920 specifically for a nonstop flight between the west and east coasts of the USA. The Cloudster was beaten to this milestone by a Fokker T-2, and was then sold to Claude Ryan, who adapted the aeroplane as a 10-seat passenger transport. The Cloudster was destroyed in 1926 after landing on a beach at Tijuana in Mexico after a charter flight with a consignment of beer!

Below: The Douglas DC-4E of 1938 can be categorized as too much airliner appearing too soon. For its time this transport prototype was extremely advanced, but features such as the retractable tricycle landing gear, power-boosted controls, an auxiliary power unit, air-conditioning and cabin pressurization were just slightly too far ahead of their time and the DC-4E was not placed in production even though it was typical of the type of airliner that became standard after World War II.

The end of World War I in November 1918 found the warring nations in possession of large numbers of long-range airplanes, and these soon proved an ideal starting point for air-mail and passenger services, needed by governments to send representatives swiftly and reliably to many parts of Europe in the difficult process of cleaning up the political mess of the war. The first regular international air-mail service, inaugurated even before the formal end of World War I, started in March 1918, operating between Vienna in Austria and Kiev in the Ukraine via three other cities, and lasted until November 1918. The Allied powers had a similar need after the war, and soon the skies over western Europe were buzzing with converted military airplanes transporting government officials and military officers.

The Aviation Traders Carvair was a simple British adaptation of the Douglas DC-4 airliner with a hinged nose to allow the loading of automobiles for short-range ferry flights. To provide straight-in access for the vehicles, the flightdeck was relocated to a position above the fuselage with an extended rear section that provided additional passenger accommodation.

The first genuine civil air service of a sustained nature was started in February 1919 by Deutsche Luft-Reederei, on the route between Berlin and Weimar, the old and new capitals of Germany, and was used by government officials and businessmen. Other nations were quick to get into the airline business, using wartime de Havilland, Handley Page, Breguet, and Farman bombers, converted into passenger airplanes by the conversion of their fuselages into cabins carrying wicker seats, and fitted with transparent panels on their sides to provide light and to allow the passengers to watch the progress of their flight. The cost of these services was high, and their reliability somewhat low, but they did help to pave the way for future developments toward an airline industry that was increasingly able to offer safety, reliability and increasing levels of comfort, at reduced operating costs that made the service attractive to passengers, yet still allowed the operator to make a profit. While these early commercial operations were starting in the more advanced and densely populated parts of the Western world, aviation enthusiasts were starting to make record long-distance flights to many remote parts of the world; thereby

Below: The Douglas DC-4 was one of the great airliners of the period after World War II. The type was basically a civil version of the C-54 Skymaster military transport developed in World War II as a version of the type Douglas proposed to replace the over-ambitious DC-4E, and itself paved the way for the more capable DC-6, and DC-7 airliners that helped confirm that long-range air routes, including those across major oceans, were both practical and economical.

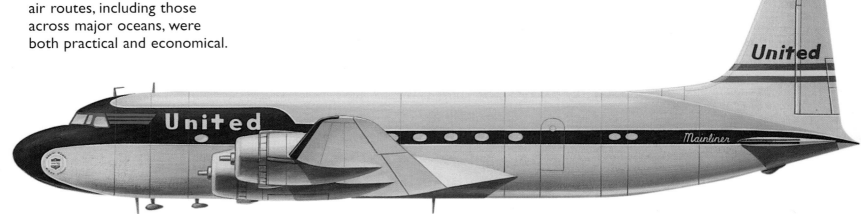

paving the way for the later emergence of long-range commercial service that were initially designed to link Europe with the colonial empires of countries such as the UK, France, Italy, and the Netherlands. The newspapers of the 1920s were important sponsors of these long-distance record-breaking efforts, which helped to spur the development of aircraft that could carry useful loads over considerable distances and with great reliability. The record-breaking flights across the North and South Atlantic, from North America to South America, and from Europe to Africa, the Middle East, the Far East, and Australasia were enormous achievements for the men and women who made them. Just as importantly, they opened the possibility of scheduled flights by examining the likely routes and locating spots suitable for the establishment of staging post airfields on the best of them.

The 1920s were years of considerable expansion, but this expansion took place in a completely disorganized manner. There was little regulation of the airlines, and only rudimentary certificates of airworthiness for their airplanes. The result was the sudden emergence of many airlines with only the flimsiest of financial backing, and the development of airliners was undertaken on such a haphazard basis that many were doomed before entering service. The overall result was a boom in the airline business and the industries supporting it. Unfortunately, however it was all very much like a bubble that could easily burst, and this happened with great frequency to companies during the 1920s. Germany was a case in point: by the early 1920s, there were many small German airlines, which either failed or were amalgamated into two major companies, Deutsche Aero Lloyd and Junkers Luftverkehr. Even these companies required subsidies from the government, and as the mid-1920s depression deepened, the government forced an amalgamation of the two companies into Deutsche Luft Hansa (later Deutsche Lufthansa), which later became the German national carrier.

The Mitsubishi MC-20 was the civil version of the Ki-57 military transport of World War II, and both types were therefore derivatives of the Ki-21, which was one of the Imperial Japanese army air force's primary heavy bombers. The type could carry 11 passengers in addition to its crew of four, and by the standards of the day, was a capable and economic light transport.

Below: The Sud-Est SE.161 Languedoc was a French airliner of the period immediately after World War II, and could carry a crew of four, and between 33 and 44 passengers, according to the density of the cabin layout. The type was a simple derivative of the Bloch MB.162 heavy bomber, and although initially placed in service with Gnome-Rhüne radial engines, the comparatively few examples of this visually interesting type were later revised with Pratt & Whitney radial engines.

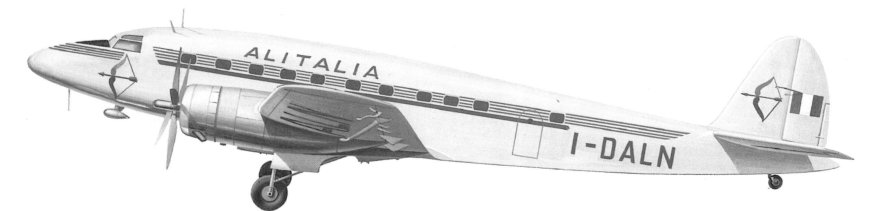

The same process was typical in other European countries up to the late 1930s, resulted in one or two national carriers (for short/medium- and long-haul routes) and a number of small private companies to maintain subsidiary scheduled and air charter services. Prices were generally high, limiting the availability of air transport to the wealthy, and although airlines could offer their passengers considerable comfort, they realized that the growth of their European trade was limited by the continent's relatively small size and the existence of good road and rail communications that could often provide a cheaper, and sometimes a faster, 'service.'

For this reason, many European companies found a commercial logic in a diversification into airline operations in the world's less developed countries, where comparatively greater size and poorer surface communications made airline operations more practical and attractive in purely commercial terms, and particularly where a country was being opened up for development with modern financial and industrial institutions. Belgium, France, Italy, the Netherlands and the UK all had empires in which separate countries could be linked by long-range routes and opened up by shorter-range routes, especially within the more backward countries with few large urban centers otherwise connected only by poor surface communications. Germany opted to develop ties with South American countries and with China, and the USSR made enormous and largely successful efforts to link minor as well as major points within its own huge land

The Savoia-Marchetti SM.95 made its first flight some four months before the Italian government's September 1943 armistice with the Allies during World War II. After World War II a small batch of 12 aircraft was completed to provide Italian air lines with a medium transport for the resumption of civil services in Europe. The SM.95 carried a crew of four and up to 18 passengers, and was to be seen with a number of different four-engined powerplants.

Below: Stemming from design work undertaken in some secrecy during World War II, the Sud-Ouest SO.30 Bretagne was a portly French transport that first flew in February 1945, and was later built in modest numbers. The type was delivered in freighter and passenger models, the latter with accommodation for a crew of five and up to 43 passengers, and these variants were powered by the Pratt & Whitney R-2800 Double Wasp and Gnome-Rhûne 14R-81 radial engines respectively.

The only powered aeroplane design by de Havilland Australia to reach production status (a mere 20 aircraft), the DHA-3 Drover was a rugged utility transport first flown in 1948, with a powerplant of three de Havilland Gipsy Major 10 inline engines. The type could carry a crew of two and up to eight passengers, and the production aircraft were used by Qantas, the Australian national airline, and by the Royal Flying Doctor Service, which phased its last aircraft out of service during 1970.

mass with airline operations. The Soviet effort was made initially with German technical support, but soon began to develop great impetus of its own, as the Soviets started the development of specialized transport aircraft that could operate in the nation's widely differing climates and geographical regions.

In many of the more backward areas, it was not passengers but freight loads that were the mainstay of airline operations, and here the Germans and Dutch scored with a number of important airliners and freight transports. The Germans were quick to appreciate the importance of all-metal construction for long-term durability as well as general reliability under adverse operating conditions, and their series of Junkers transports, most notably the F 13 and then the W 33 and W 34, all based on corrugated metal construction and with monoplane rather than biplane layout, were important both in the history of air transport and in building up Germany's airplane industry, at a time when the country was banned from developing or owning military airplanes. The Fokker company in the Netherlands used the type of structure that it had pioneered for fighters in Germany during World War I: a slab-sided but capacious fuselage of plywood- and fabric-covered welded steel tube construction was carried by a high-set wing of plywood-covered wooden construction with a section so thick that no external bracing was needed. These basic concepts were developed for single- or multi-engine powerplants as the requirements dictated, the classic example being the F.VII that was built as the single-engined F.VII and three-engined F.VIII-3m. The combination of great strength with lack of struts and rigging wires marked an impor-

tant advance for the Germans and Dutch over the British and French machines of the day, which were slow and clumsy airplanes, built in small numbers for the particular needs of national carriers rather than as purely commercial airliners with export potential.

The major airliner-producing countries also built many types of commercial flying boat, almost always in small numbers. These were used on the long-distance routes to the European countries' overseas empires, and made extensive use of the sea, lakes and rivers to overcome the lack of airfields for landplanes. Although slow, these flying boats offered unparalleled comfort. The most popular period for these flying boats was the 1930s, and by this time the European flying boats (Breguet, Dornier, Latécoère, and Short types for the most part) were matched by some classic machines from American manufacturers such as Boeing, Consolidated, Martin, and Sikorsky. The Boeing and Martin flying boats were designed mainly for the long over-water routes being pioneered across the Pacific and the Atlantic, while the Consolidated and Sikorsky boats were more frequently used over the Caribbean on the flights that linked North and South America, in the hands of what soon became Pan American Airways.

The Short Sandringham was a transport flying boat produced in small numbers after World War II as conversions of surplus Sunderland maritime reconnaissance flying boats, and these 30 or so 'boats were some of the last such machines to operate scheduled airline services. The type carried a maximum of 45 passengers on two decks.

Below: Designed by Miles aircraft before its was absorbed into the Handley Page organization, the Marathon was a British attempt of the period after World War II to create a utility light transport with a powerplant of four low-powered, but reliable, and economical de Havilland Gipsy Queen inline engines. The type could carry up to 22 passengers, and after the two leading British airlines had canceled their orders for the type, the Royal Air Force took 28 of the type as trainers while the other 12 were operated as transports by a number of export customers.

Germany tried to resurrect its pre-World War I success with airships for long-range commercial operations. Some classic flights were made by the new Zeppelin airships, which combined very long range with an unparalleled degree of comfort, but the effort ended in 1937 when the hydrogen-filled Hindenburg caught fire and crashed while attempting to land at Lakehurst, New Jersey, after a transatlantic flight. The UK also tried its hand with commercial airship operations, but was even less successful than Germany.

Air transport in the USA during most of the 1920s had been limited to air mail, and by 1926, the original army-operated service had been replaced by a vast network operated by no fewer than 400 companies flying large numbers of airplanes. Payment was made by the Post Office on the basis of the weight of mail carried, which encouraged the development of small, high-speed airplanes. In 1930, the basis of payment was changed from weight to volume, which led immediately to larger airplanes that could carry fare-paying passengers in any space not full of mail, generating additional revenue for

Top and above: Rivaling the Douglas DC-4, DC-6 and DC-7 series in technical capability, exceeding it in esthetic attraction, but never equaling its commercial success, the Lockheed Constellation, Super Constellation and Starliner series can justly be said to have marked the apogee of piston-engined airliner development. Both these aircraft are L-1049 Super Constellation transports.

the company. The early air-mail services had established large numbers of viable routes across the USA and had prompted the development of airfields and navigational techniques, and the development of a full-scale airline industry was rapid as soon as the economic situation and regulatory framework permitted. To meet the early demand, Fokker airplanes were imported and built in the USA under license, while purely American designs included the Ford Tri-Motor monoplane, the Curtiss Condor twin-engine biplane, and the Boeing Model 80 three-engine biplane.

In the early 1930s, the technological revolution in airplane design led to a pair of classic airliners that immediately pushed the USA to the fore of the airliner business, and therefore in the vanguard of the airline business. These new airliners introduced the low-wing monoplane layout, with an enclosed cockpit, retractable landing gear, smooth stressed-skin construction in metal with fabric limited to the covering of the control surfaces, and a number of other advanced features such as cabin air conditioning and powerful engines with variable-pitch propellers. The first of these two epoch-making airliners was the Boeing Model 247 that entered service in 1933. The Model 247 was an immense achievement at the technical level, but it was sized to the exact requirements of the airline run by Boeing's parent company. This meant that the Model 247 lacked the customer appeal of the DC-1, produced in competition by Douglas and with the ability to carry a larger passenger load. The DC-1 was basically a prototype that was soon evolved into the moderately successful DC-2, and then into the hugely successful DC-3. The DC-3 was larger than the Model 247, had trailing-edge flaps to provide the low take-off and landing speeds that promoted safety and allowed the use of small airports, and was economical to buy and operate. It is impossible to exaggerate the importance of the DC-3: by 1939, at least 90

The Vickers Vanguard was designed to capitalize on the considerable market niche secured by the Viscount, which was the world's first airliner with a turboprop powerplant. But despite its several good qualities, it never secured large-scale orders at a time when airlines were attracted more strongly by the new turbojet-powered airliners that had greater passenger appeal. The Vanguard saw only modest service in its original passenger form, most of the aircraft were then revised for longer service as Merchantman freighters.

Designed as an interim type that could provide employment for the company, and an effective short/medium-range transport for British airlines seeking to re-establish themselves after World War II, the Vickers VC-1 Viking was a modest commercial success.

per cent of the world's air traffic was being carried in DC-3s, and to meet military requirements during World War II, the C-47 Skytrain (or Dakota) version was evolved and built in vast numbers as the backbone of the Allies' air transport and airborne forces capabilities. By the end of World War II, more than 10,000 of this basic design had been produced.

The 455 DC-3s built before the United States' entry in World War II had marked the beginning of a new era in safe, reliable air transport for ordinary men and women as well as for the wealthy, and this tendency continued in the period after World War II as thousands of ex-military transports flooded onto the commercial market. Airlines operating the DC-3 sprang up all over the world, and the DC-3 can be credited with the creation of the world airline consciousness in the late 1940s and early 1950s. Even in the mid-1990s there are several hundred still flying in many parts of the world.

The Europeans tried to match the US achievements with aircraft such as the Junkers Ju 52/3m, which was a three-engined airplane with Junkers' favored corrugated skinning and fixed main landing gear units, but none of their efforts succeeded. By the mid-1930s, the threat of war over Europe was urging the development of military rather than civil airplanes. Germany produced the four-engined Focke-Wulf Fw 200 Condor as a potential land-based transatlantic airliner at the time as the British and Americans were concentrating on the Short 'C' and 'G' class and the Boeing Model 314 flying boats for the same task, while the British produced a number of medium-range airliners of generally obsolescent design. All of them were overtaken by the rush to war.

The Americans had another two years of peace ahead of them, and this factor allowed them to consolidate their already considerable lead in the airliner and airline businesses. The DC-3 marked an important turning point in this process, for the airplane's reliability and high

The Douglas DC-4 lacked the elegance of the rival Lockheed Constellation, but was a thoroughly workmanlike and reliable medium/long-range transport that enjoyed the commercial advantages of being a development of the C-54 military transport that had been built in large numbers during World War II, and which was therefore comparatively cheap to produce as conversions of surplus C-54s.

The Ilyushin Il-14 was a Soviet attempt to create a successor to the classic Douglas DC-3 airliner, which it had built before and during World War II as the PS-84 (later Lisunov Li-2). The Il-14 was a practical, but uninspired, design that secured orders only from the USSR and those countries that formed its 'empire' during the 1940s and 1950s.

performance showed that a plateau had been reached in the development of airliners with piston engines, each rated at up to about 1,200 hp. Here the American companies had an important advantage in the radial piston engines designed and manufactured by Pratt & Whitney and Wright. These offered high reliability and a good power-to-weight ratio in families such as the Pratt & Whitney R-985 Wasp Junior and Wright R-975 Whirlwind series with a rating in the order of 500 to 600hp, and the Pratt & Whitney R-1830 Twin Wasp and Wright R-1820 Cyclone series with a rating in the order of 1,000 to 1,200hp. The reliability of these engines also made it possible to schedule far more regular flights, until it became clear that scheduled flights were at the mercy of the poor weather that often extended up to 20,000ft, about 5,000ft above the airliners' normal cruising altitude.

The obvious solution was to fly above this altitude, where the airliners would suffer less from adverse weather: such operations also opened the possibility of faster cruising flight because of the reduced air pressure. This important objective was difficult to attain with the technological standards of the late 1930s, because it required cabin pressurization and more effective supercharging of the engines. Pressurization was required to avoid the difficulties and dangers of anoxia (lack of oxygen) on the passengers and crew as a result of the lower air pressures of high-altitude flight, and better supercharging was needed to maintain the power output of the engines at their rated figures despite the fall in air pressure and thus the reduced amount of oxygen that would be available to be mixed with the fuel and burned in the engine cylinders. If these problems could be solved, there was the accompanying need for better navigation and an automatic pilot to relieve the flight crew of the tiring routine on the type of long-distance flights that would become feasible. Determined efforts into all these features were made on both sides of the Atlantic during the 1930s, but it was the technologically ambitious American companies which came up with most of the answers and then had two additional years of peace to develop their ideas into an acceptable hardware form.

As it was, the United States' entry into World War II in 1941 curtailed these efforts before they had reached fruition. The Douglas DC-4E and Lockheed L-49 Constellation airliners each had most of these features, as well as tricycle landing gear to keep the fuselage level on the ground, but the DC-4E was plagued by development problems and the Constellation was too late to enter production before it was overtaken by the war. The demands of the war led to considerable development in all these fields, however, and the DC-4E was superseded by the simpler but unpressurized C-54 military transport that re-emerged from the war as the DC-4 long-range airliner.

During the course of the war, only the Americans and British required a very large air transport capability using modern aircraft, although the Germans and Soviets also possessed major transport arms operating older and therefore less capable airplanes. The Allied demand for transport airplanes was met almost entirely from US design and production sources, further increasing the American dominance of the air transport scene after the war. Radial engines offering up to 3,500hp became common and allowed the development of airliner families of growing size and capability. The DC-4 was followed by the pressurized DC-6 and the more capable DC-7 series, while the L-49 emerged from military service in a number of supremely elegant Constellation, Super Constellation and Starliner versions of very high performance and huge customer appeal. Boeing sought to get into the act with its Model 377 Stratocruiser, a development of the wartime B-29 Superfortress strategic bomber, but it was produced in smaller quantities than the Douglas and Lockheed types. The British and French attempted to break back into the long-haul airliner market without real success; their airliners were based too solidly on wartime technology.

The Sud-Est SE.161 Languedoc was evolved as the MB.161 in parallel with the Bloch MB.162 bomber during World War II, and the civil transport was initially ordered by the occupying Germans in the war. Although no aircraft were completed until after the Germans had been expelled from France in 1944. Both the bomber and the transport were conceptual derivatives of the MB.160 short-range transport designed before the war, and the Languedoc saw limited airline service in the late 1940s and early 1950s.

Much the same applied in the field of shorter-range airliners, whose market was dominated or even saturated by surplus DC-3s. The growing sophistication of the airline market in the late 1940s persuaded some manufacturers that customers might prefer greater performance and comfort than could be provided by the DC-3; this conviction led to the Convair CV-240 and the Martin 2-0-2 series. The CV-240 was a thoroughly modern design with high performance and full pressurization for great passenger comfort; it was succeeded by fairly large numbers of the improved CV-340 and CV-440 models. All three types are still in service, often with turboprop engines in place of the original two radial engines. The Martin 2-0-2 was less successful, and even the improved Martin 4-0-4 secured only small orders.

The British sought to break into this exceptionally tricky market with airliners such as the Vickers VC-1 Viking. This attempt failed, though greater success was won by smaller short-range types such as the de Havilland D.H.104 Dove twin-engined and D.H.114 Heron four-engined models. They served mainly as feederliners carrying

Above: The Yakovlev Yak-42 first flew in 1975 as a short-range airliner for Aeroflot, the Soviet national airline, and has a powerplant of three turbofans located at the tail.

passengers from smaller airfields into main airports where they could pick up long-haul flights. These two British airplanes also helped to pave the way for modern corporate transports; a large number were bought by major companies for transporting senior executives.

The Soviets had produced the DC-3 under license as the Lisunov Li-2, and it was extensively used after the war, when it was joined, but never replaced, by slightly more modern airliners such as the Ilyushin Il-12 and Il-14.

During World War II, the British had fielded the only Allied operational jet fighter of the war, the Gloster Meteor, and were well advanced with a number of gas turbine engines such as turbojets and turboprops of the fat centrifugal-flow and slim axial-flow types. The Americans were making progress, which speeded up as the implications of German research and manufacture were relized. But in the mid- and late 1940s, the British held a lead which the govern-

Above: The BAC One-Eleven pioneered the powerplant arrangement of two turbofans attached to the rear fuselage below the T-tail, and was a design that deserved better than the modest sales success it finally secured.

ment and the airplane and engine manufacturing companies realized could be turned to profit. The world was already being effectively shrunk by the speed and range of the long-haul airliners flying into a growing number of major airports in most parts of the world. The desire of the ever-increasing number of passengers for higher-speed comfort rather than lower-speed luxury could best be met by jet-powered airliners that could be half as fast again as piston-engined airplanes. Other 'pluses' for the gas turbine engine in comparison with

Below: Built in larger numbers than any other airliner in history, the Boeing Model 737 is a short/medium-range type that has been built in many variants during a long production and development career, which is still continuing in the mid-1990s. This is an example of the Model 737-200 that was the first variant built in large numbers.

the reciprocating piston engine were its mechanical simplicity and lower vibration, which was thought to offer additional advantages of greater reliability and better passenger acceptance.

The two airplanes that pioneered the concept were the Vickers VC-2 Viscount and the de Havilland D.H.106 Comet. The Viscount was a medium-capacity type designed for short and medium ranges with four turboprop engines, and the Comet was another medium-capacity type, designed for medium to long ranges with four turbojet engines. Initial acceptance in the early 1950s was slow, but once passengers began to appreciate the advantages of the new airliners' speed and vibration-free comfort, demand began to swell considerably. The Viscount went on to notch up some 450 sales, including a large number in the US The Comet looked set to match this growth in sales until it suffered two crashes: the cause was found to be metal fatigue, and the redesign of the problem areas coincided with a decision to upgrade the model for nonstop transatlantic operations. The delay was so great that, by the time it was ready for service, it had been overtaken by two new American types. These were the Boeing Model 707 and

Below: The Fokker F28 Fellowship was designed in the early 1960s as a twin-turbofan airliner to carry about 50 passengers over short/medium-range routes, and as such to serve as a partner for the Dutch company's F27 Friendship short-range airliner with a powerplant of two turboprop engines.

Douglas DC-8, which marked a decisive turning point in airline operations. The two aircraft were similar in layout, with four turbojet engines in pods under the wings and well-swept flying surfaces for high speed. They were also designed for availability as models tailored to the exact requirements of any customer. Boeing achieved this

Left: The Douglas DC-8 was designed to rival the Boeing Model 707 medium/long-range airliner. With a powerplant of four turbojet engines in pods mounted below and ahead of the wing's swept leading edges. The DC-8 never achieved the huge sales success of the Model 707, but was nonetheless built in large numbers with a turbojet and later a turbofan powerplant, and many of the aircraft remain in service mainly as freighters.

aim better than Douglas, and for this reason, the Model 707 sold better than the DC-8. Unlike the British, who preferred to design their jet airliners (the Comet and the later Vickers VC-10) with large wings to suit existing airfields, the Americans gambled successfully that the appeal of their faster aircraft would force airports to extend their runways rather than lose business.

The Model 707 and the DC-8 were later adapted for greater range and payload with fuel-economical turbofan engines, and from the early 1970s began to enjoy a second career as freighters, as they were replaced in passenger service by more advanced types. Both aircraft led to a whole series of jetliners that have consolidated the US position as the world's most important manufacturer of airliners. The Model 707 was followed by the Model 727 three-jet short/medium-range medium-capacity airliner, the Model 737 twin-jet short-range small-capacity airliner, the Model 747 'Jumbo' four-jet long-range high-capacity airliner, the Model 757 twin-jet equivalent to the Model 727, the Model 767 twin-jet medium-range high-capacity airliner, and finally the Model 777 twin-jet airliner that entered service in the mid-1990s. The Douglas (now McDonnell Douglas) series followed the DC-8 with the DC-9 twin-jet medium-range small-capacity airliner that has been upgraded as the MD-80 and MD-90 series, and the DC-10 three-jet long-range medium/large-capacity airliner that has been upgraded as the MD-11. The only other US airliner of the period worthy of note was the Lockheed L-1011 TriStar, a three-jet in the same basic class as the DC-10. All could be supplied as passenger airplanes, or as freighters, or as mixed passenger/freight airplanes, or even as convertible passenger/freight airplanes, thereby increasing the flexibility of the operating airline in

Above: First flown in July 1960 as a regional airliner with a rectangular-section fuselage and a powerplant of two Turbomeca Bastan turboprops, the Holste MH.260 was produced only in very small numbers and was then passed to Nord-Aviation for development as the N.262 with a pressurized circular-section fuselage.

Below: The Douglas DC-9 was designed as a short/medium-range airliner to complement the DC-8, and as such was a rival to the Boeing Model 737.

Below: The Fokker F27 Friendship is an unspectacular but thoroughly practical and economical light transport for the movement of limited numbers of passengers over short ranges. Like its turbofan-powered partner, the F28 Fellowship, the F27 was radically updated in the 1980s to re-emerge as the F50.

Below: The BAe 146, now known as the Avro Regional Jet, was designed by Hawker Siddeley. Postponed before the construction of a single aeroplane, and then revived after the absorption of Hawker Siddeley into British Aerospace. The type has a powerplant of four turbofans for reliability of operation on short/medium-range routes, and is still selling adequately if not with spectacular success.

meeting exact markets and generating income.

Small niches were filled by other Western airliners such as the Lockheed L-188 Electra four-turboprop type, the Fokker F.27 Friendship twin-turboprop and F.28 Fellowship twin-jet types that were later upgraded to suit modern operating conditions as the F50 and F100 respectively, the BAC One-Eleven twin-jet type, and the Hawker Siddeley Trident three-jet type. The Soviets produced their own airliners paralleling the Western airplanes, but these Antonov, Ilyushin, and Tupolev turboprop and turbojet models were technically inferior to the Western airplanes and thus considerably less economical to operate. This fact thwarted their export sale to any but Soviet-aligned countries. Before the collapse of the communist system in the late 1980s, marked by the disappearance of the USSR and the emergence of the Commonwealth of Independent States, the USSR had begun to move toward the creation of more modern airliners that would be able to compete on more level terms with the Western counterparts, and this effort continues in the mid-1990s even though it is strongly hampered by the economic problems of Russia and its fellow states in the CIS.

The British and French sought to break into what was becoming an American monopoly with the technically superb Aérospatiale/British Aerospace Concorde, a low-capacity supersonic transport that has acquired a magnificent reputation on the 'blue ribbon' transatlantic routes, but failed to secure more than a handful of sales. The Soviets produced their own Tupolev Tu-144 that was dubbed 'Concordski' by the Western press, but this type was withdrawn from service after serious problems had been encountered.

Below: The Tupolev Tu-134 was designed in the early 1960s, and was evolved as a somewhat modified and scaled-down derivative of the Tu-124, itself an adaptation of the Tu-104 airliner, which was the first Soviet transport of the jet-powered type.

Europe's effort to grab a larger slice of the airline pie led to the formation of Airbus Industrie by Aérospatiale in France, British Aerospace in the UK, CASA in Spain and MBB (now part of Deutsche Aerospace) in Germany, with Fokker of the Netherlands as an associate. This major consortium has pressed ahead with the development of several important airliners to compete with Boeing and McDonnell Douglas. The A300, A310, and A320 are already well established in service, while the A330 and A340 entered service in the 1990s. The pricing of these European airplanes had led to disputes with US manufacturers, but the technical excellence of the airliners has helped them to break into the entrenched US position on a global basis, including their selection by several major US airlines in preference to airliners of American manufacture.

The cost and long lead times of aerospace developments have made modern airliner families very long-lived. Individual airplanes serve for many years, and the basic design is always planned as a starting point for development with longer or shorter fuselages, modified wings, more powerful engines, a choice of engine types, an extra landing gear unit to allow greater weight, additional fuel, and a host of electronic modifications. So, even if the latest version of an airliner

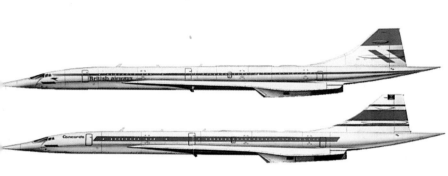

Above: The result of an Anglo-French collaboration and currently the world's only supersonic airliner, the Aérospatiale/BAe Concorde is surely one of the most exciting and elegant transports ever built.

Below: The McDonnell Douglas MD-11, here seen in the marking of Swissair, the Swiss national carrier, is an updated development of the DC-10 with a powerplant of three turbofans installed as one in the base of the vertical tail surface and two under the wings. A notable development evident here is the use of wing-tip 'winglets,' which reduce drag and thereby boost cruising range.

looks very similar to the first variant, it can be a very different airplane in its detail and performance. This versatility of design also helps sales, for adaptation can readily be produced to meet the detailed requirement of any customer prepared to order it.

New technology is currently transforming the airliner once more. The shape of the most modern airliner may not be very different from that of the 1970s, but composite materials, computer-controlled flight systems, advanced engines, and other cybernetic features are all extensively used to increase safety, reduce weight, and allow operation by a smaller crew. Performance has reached a plateau, so the emphasis in the latest airliners is placed on economy of operation combined with maximum safety.

It is difficult to predict the path that commercial aviation will follow in the future, especially as there has been a decline in passenger demand since the mid-1980s, and many airliners, some of them fairly modern and economical types, have been 'mothballed' in areas such as the deserts of the American south-west. There can be little doubt that passenger demand will increase once more, but the airline industry is faced by two major problems. These are the extraordinarily high cost of purchasing and running modern airliners, which places a great

Airbus Industrie was created in 1967 as a European design and manufacturing consortium that could rival the capabilities of the three American aerospace giants, namely Boeing, Lockheed, and McDonnell Douglas. The first Airbus product was the A300, a twin-turbofan airliner of the wide-body type optimized for the medium-range role, and seen here in the form of an A300B4 of Olympic Airways, the Greek national carrier.

Below: The Sud Est Caravelle was the first of France's jet-powered airliners. The Caravelle was also the first airliner to have its engines pod-mounted on the sides of the rear fuselage.

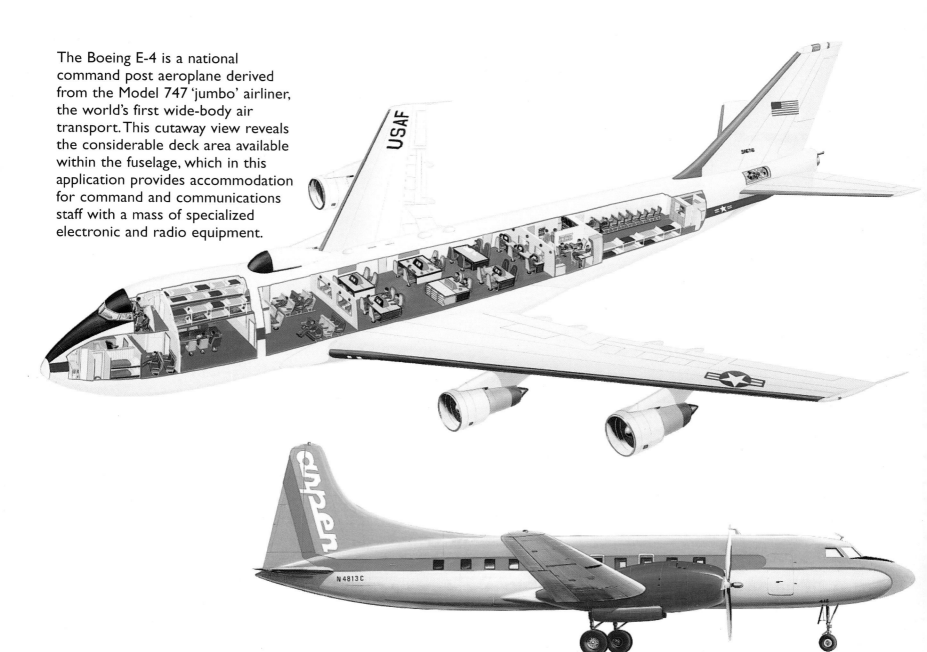

The Boeing E-4 is a national command post aeroplane derived from the Model 747 'jumbo' airliner, the world's first wide-body air transport. This cutaway view reveals the considerable deck area available within the fuselage, which in this application provides accommodation for command and communications staff with a mass of specialized electronic and radio equipment.

Above right: The Convair CV-240 was the most successful of the American airliners designed after World War II as successors to the Douglas DC-3, and was later developed into the improved CV-340 and CV-440 models. Several of these aircraft remain in service, many of them revised with a turboprop powerplant. Typical of these later is the CV-580 with two Allison 501 engines, and the ability to carry 56 passengers over a range of 2,250 miles at a cruising speed of 340 mph.

emphasis on even the slightest of operating economies that can be implemented, and a strengthening environmental lobby that wishes to see no increase in the number of airplane movements into and out of airports, or any extension of the hours during which commercial operators may use airports in urban areas. The effect must surely be to spur the development of airliners that are larger yet quieter. The additional size will mean the movement of more passengers without extra flights, and quietening of the engines will help the airliners to meet the most strident demands of the environmental lobby. Hand-in-hand with fundamental and obvious changes will come other alterations that will be just as fundamental but considerably less obvious. This latter category of changes will include engines that run more economically and cleanly to burn a reduced quantity of fuel per unit of thrust, airframes that exploit all the latest developments in structural and aerodynamic thinking to reduce airframe weight and improve operating efficiency, and computer systems that boost productivity while also enhancing safety.

Helicopters

As can be seen from the the previous chapter, the progress made by fixed-wing airplanes since the Wright brothers' successful first powered flight in December 1903 has been enormous, and has without doubt altered the course of the 20th century out of all recognition. Yet the technical development of the helicopter since 1939 has been even more impressive, and if the helicopter has failed to secure the same popularity and world-shattering importance as the fixed-wing airplane, this is a reflection of its particular and more limited task in life.

Yet what is a helicopter? The clue is given most clearly by an alternative term, rotary-wing airplane. All wings create lift by moving through the air, which is divided at the leading edge to flow round the shape of the wing section from front to rear before joining again at the trailing edge. The upper surface is generally longer than the lower surface, and this reduces the pressure of the air flowing over it: nature hates any difference in pressure, and the higher pressure under the wing pushes upward to try to equalize itself with the lower pressure over the wing, in the process pushing the wing up (or, looked at in a different way, creating 'lift') and thus allowing the airplane to fly. The whole process needs moving air, and in a fixed-wing airplane this means that the machine must move forward through the air and also, in all but very rare circumstances of high wind speeds, over the ground as well. This is why fixed-wing airplanes need large airports with their long runways: these allow the airplane to accelerate to or

Designed by Sud-Aviation before its incorporation into Aérospatiale, the SA 315B Lama was a development of the Alouette turbine-powered helicopter to meet the particular requirement of the Indian armed forces, which needed a utility helicopter able to operate successfully under 'hot and high' conditions. The Lama can lift four passengers or a slung load of 2,500 lb, and can hover in ground effect at an altitude of 12,300 ft. The Lama also holds the world's absolute height record for helicopters at 40,820 ft, and has made the highest take-offs and landing ever recorded at an altitude of 24,600 ft.

Top: The MBB BO105 is a German twin-turbine utility helicopter that had been developed in several variants for the military as well as civil markets.

Above center: The Sikorsky S-76 first flew in May 1977, and is an advanced civil helicopter with a twin-turbine powerplant, fully retractable tricycle landing gear, and provision for up to 12 passengers carried in a moderately large cabin.

Above: The Aérospatiale Dauphin series was designed as successor to the classic Alouette III helicopter family, and has been produced in a wide assortment of civil and military variants with a powerplant of one or two turboshafts, fixed or retractable landing gear, and a fenestron tail rotor enclosed in the vertical tail surface.

decelerate from the speed through the air at which their wings will create enough lift to support the whole machine.

The helicopter or rotary-wing airplane, on the other hand, creates the required lift by whirling an assembly of long, narrow wings (blades) around a vertical shaft, so creating movement through the air, with the complete machine stationary relative to the ground: this means that the helicopter can take off and land vertically, in the process doing away with the need for runways, and also hover in the air. The word helicopter is derived from two Greek words, helix meaning spiral and pteron meaning wing, and the combination neatly describes how the machine works. The power needed for this process is greater than that required for a fixed-wing airplane of similar weight, and one of the greatest limitations in the development of rotary-wing flight is this unavoidable problem: power for power, there is no way that a rotary-wing airplane can match a fixed-wing airplane for speed or load-carrying capability.

The blades of the rotor can be altered in pitch (the angle of the blade to the ambient airflow) all together by the pilot's collective pitch control to change the amount of lift created by the rotor, so allowing the helicopter to rise or descend as desired. The pilot also has a cyclic pitch control to alter the angle of the whole rotor relative to the fuselage: tilting the rotor forward allows the rotor to pull the helicopter forward and create movement over the ground. Tilting of the rotor disc in the forward direction produces forward flight, and the rotor can also be tilted to either side or backwards, allowing flight in these directions. In most helicopters, namely those machines with a single main rotor, the turning of the main rotor creates a torque reaction that tends to rotate the fuselage in the opposite direction to the main rotor, and this tendency is controlled by the tail rotor. This is a small unit located near the tail, turning on a horizontal shaft to act as a side-facing propeller that cancels out the tendency of the fuselage to swing in the opposite direction to the main rotor: the tail

rotor is controllable to act as a rudder and so allowing the pilot to 'point' the helicopter in the direction he wants. All in all, the piloting of a helicopter is not as natural as the piloting of a fixed-wing airplane, and requires special training.

Yet its maneuverability without forward air speed is what gives the helicopter its most useful capabilities, and we are all aware of the helicopter's unique ability to operate into and out of small spaces such as the roofs of buildings, forest clearings, the decks of ships, and oil rig platforms, all of which are inaccessible to fixed-wing airplanes. Just as important is the ability of the helicopter to fly into areas too rough or too soft for the creation of a conventional fixed-wing airplane landing strip: the sides of mountains, broken ground, sandy deserts and even the sea are areas that spring to mind in this regard.

The advantages of the helicopter suggest the reason why men have dreamt of such machines since as he time of Leonardo da Vinci in the second half of the 15th century. At the same time, the power requirement and complexity of such machines explains why it was 1939 before the first practical helicopter was developed, by Igor Sikorsky. This is not to suggest that there had not been a multitude of helicopter designs in the interval. None of these could possibly have come to anything before the invention of the internal-combustion engine in 1885, and its development to a practical level for airplanes by about 1900, before the introduction of a wealth of experimental helicopters. The first of these to achieve any real success was a French twin-rotor machine by Paul Cornu, which in November 1907 achieved the first man-carrying free flight by a helicopter: it lifted its pilot to a height of 1ft for about 20 seconds. Other notable helicopter pioneers were the Dane J C Ellehammer, the Englishmen B R Benen, E R Mumford and Louis Brennan, the French team of Louis Breguet and Professor Richet, the Dutchman von Baumhauer, the Frenchman Paul Oehmichen, the Austro-Hungarian Otto von Karman, the French-domiciled Argentine Raoul Pescara, the Americans G de Bothezat and Henry Berliner, and the Russians Sikorsky (who later emigrated to the USA, Boris Yuriev, I P Bratukhin and several others.

First flown in 1971 and delivered from 1976, the Agusta A 109 utility helicopter was planned for the highest possible performance without the use of enormously powerful engines, and therefore had an advanced four-blade main rotor, a powerplant of two turboshafts installed in a neat faring behind, and to each side of the main rotor pylon, and fully retractable tricycle landing gear. Accommodation is provided for eight, and the type can also be adapted for a host of paramilitary and military applications, with a roof-mounted sight and an external load-carrying beam fitted with hardpoints for weapons of several different types.

None of these men achieved the aim of a practical helicopter, but most of them were important innovators who succeeded in developing a technical feature that was essential to the creation of a workable helicopter. Oddly enough, however, the first practical rotary-wing airplane was not a helicopter but the gyroplane, developed in Spain during the early 1920s by Juan de la Cierva with the name Autogiro (modified to Autogyro for similar machines designed by other men). De la Cierva's motivation was the alarming number of crashes by fixed-wing aircraft in stalling accidents, including the fatal crash of one of de la Cierva's own fixed-wing designs. The stall occurs as the pilot pulls up the nose of the airplane to maintain lift when speed drops, and the stall proper occurs when the smooth airflow over the upper surface of the wings breaks away and becomes turbulent: the result is a steep dive as the nose drops, often accompanied by a spin. Many early airplanes were prone to a catastrophic stall with little or no warning, and at low levels this almost invariably meant a crash and loss of life.

De la Cierva reasoned that the best way to remove this problem was the use of a freely turning, or windmilling, rotor instead of the conventional wing. The Autogyro is fitted with a conventional fuselage and engine with tractor propeller, and the rotor windmills as the propeller pulls the whole machine forward. The Autogyro can take off and land in a very short distance (and take off vertically if a clutch system is used to spin up the rotor on the ground), is unstallable, descends under control if the engine fails, and has no torque problem as the rotor is unpowered. Compared with the helicopter, however, the Autogyro lacks hovering ability. Considerable strides were made with the development of the Autogyro between 1925 and the time of de la Cierva's death in an airliner crash in 1936, but the successful development of

The Aérospatiale AS 332 Super Puma Mk II, now known as a product of Eurocopter France since the 1992 merger of the helicopter division of Aérospatiale and MBB (Eurocopter Deutschland), is a development of the AS 332 Super Puma with improved rotors and a lengthened cabin to allow the insertion of an extra seat row, increasing the passenger payload from 21 to 24. The Super Puma Mk II is the civil model, and the equivalent military version is the AS 532 Cougar Mk II available in unarmed troop transport and armed multi-role variants. The Super Puma Mk II is a highly capable type, and is certificated for flight under adverse weather conditions which, in conjunction with its twin-turboshaft powerplant, makes it popular for the support of offshore resources-exploitation platforms.

the helicopter in the next few years meant the virtual death of the Autogyro until it was revived as a sporting machine in the 1960s.

In 1935, Louis Breguet re-entered the helicopter field for the first time since before World War I, collaborating with Dorand to produce the Gyroplane Laboratoire. This used twin two-blade rotors turning in opposite directions to remove torque problems, as the reaction of each unit cancelled that of the other, and in the course of several successful flights established a number of world helicopter records including a speed of 61mph, a height of 518ft. and a distance of 27.34 miles.

The Gyroplane Laboratoire was finally destroyed in an accident, and the main stream of helicopter development moved to Germany and the Focke-Wulf (later Focke-Achgelis) Fw61. This was similar to the Gyroplane Laboratoire in having two rotors turning in opposite directions so that each cancelled the other's torque, but whereas the Gyroplane Laboratoire's two rotors were placed one above the other, in the Fw61 there were located side-by-side on the end of long booms extending from the sides of the fuselage. This made the Fw61 very controllable, but also too wide on overall size for real measure of practicality. The Fw61 first flew in 1936 and established a whole new set of world records including a speed of 76 mph, a distance of 143 miles and an altitude of 11,243ft. German pioneers went on to develop a number of potentially important helicopters in the period leading up to World War II, and during the war also evolved several interesting developments including the Focke-Achgelis Fa 223 Drache (kite) general-purpose and troop transport helicopter, the Focke-Achgelis Fa 330 Bachstelze (wagtail) observation gyrokite to be towed by submarine's as a means of extending their visual horizon in the acquisition of possible targets or the detection of potential threats, and the conceptually very advanced Flettner Fl 282 Kolibri (humming bird) anti-submarine and observation helicopter with counter-rotating and intermeshing side-by-side twin rotors.

The most important pioneer of the 1930s, however, was without doubt Sikorsky, who used his own particular genius to bring together features from other helicopters for blending with his own notions to produce the world's first practical helicopter with a single main rotor. Sikorsky was the engineering manager of the United Aircraft Corporation's Vought-Sikorsky Division, and this explains the designation of this epoch-making helicopter as the VS-300, which was designed in 1938 and built early in 1939. As originally built, the VS-300 had a 75hp Lycoming engine for its single main and tail rotors, and a cyclic pitch control system. The VS-300 was first flown on 14 September 1939 while tethered to the ground and carrying stabilizing weights, and in the following test program had its cyclic pitch control system disconnected. From 13 May 1940, the tests found the VS-300 in revised form with a 90hp Franklin engine and two horizontally turning auxiliary rotors for better lateral control. The cyclic pitch con-

The largest helicopter yet flown, the Mil V-12 (or Mi-12) was a prototype machine that received the NATO reporting name 'Homer.' The V-12 set a number of impressive world records, but did not enter production or service, presumably because of intractable development problems.

trol was reconnected after modification to a fully effective form, and later additions were a tall pylon for the tail rotor, tricycle landing gear, fabric covering for the previously uncovered steel tube fuselage, and a 150hp Franklin engine. Enormous progress was made up to 1942 in a long-lasting development program, and in 1943 the VS-300 was entrusted to the Henry Ford Museum in Dearborn, Michigan.

It is impossible to overestimate the importance of the VS-300. The Gyroplane Laboratoire and Fw 61 had indeed pioneered the essential features of helicopter flight, but the VS-300 had introduced a more practical layout and the ability to carry a useful load, and had shown that the helicopter could be built with conventional construction methods for use by service pilots rather than test pilots.

By the time the VS-300 had fully proved itself, all the important airplane-manufacturing countries were embroiled in World War II. Those with a helicopter capability, namely Germany and the USA, looked for ways to use the new invention. As noted above, Germany developed the Fw 61 into the Focke-Achgelis Fa 223 Drache that was used for lifting men and supplies to outposts in mountainous regions, while the very attractive little Flettner Fl 282 Kolibri was used for shipboard reconnaissance duties in the Mediterranean and Baltic.

The German effort, although considerable in terms of a research program, failed to produce large numbers of truly effective helicopters for use in the prosecution of the war. Thus it fell to the Americans to take the bold step of first putting a helicopter into large-scale production and actually producing a significant number of machines. The helicopter involved was the VS-316A, the production derivative of the VS-300, and was known to the US military as the R-4, and to the British as the Hoverfly. The R-4 was modelled closely on the VS-300, but had a fully enclosed cabin for a crew of two, dual controls, greater power and a larger-diameter main rotor. The production run was not large, but sufficient in number to allow full testing of the helicopter in a variety of roles: the US Army Air Forces concerned themselves with the versatility and serviceability of the helicopter in geographical and climatic extremes as diverse as those of Alaska and Burma, the US Navy con-

173

Above: The Boeing/Sikorsky RAH-66 Comanche, of which the first example was completed in 1995, is an advanced multi-role helicopter for the US Army. The type has very sophisticated electronic systems for its primary scouting, target-acquisition and attack roles.

Below: The Bell Model 204 was designed in the mid-1950s as a utility helicopter with a twin-blade main rotor powered by a single turboshaft, and entered service in this form as the US Army's classic UH-1 'Huey' helicopter indelibly associated with American participation in the Vietnam War.

firmed the helicopter's ability to operate from ship platforms, the US Coast Guard proved the type's search-and-rescue (SAR) capability, and the British pioneered the type's use for reconnaissance and disaster warning. In its various forms, the R-4 was built to the extent of more than 400 helicopters. These were used in 1944 and 1945 in many of the Allies' theaters of war and, in addition to pioneering the roles mentioned above, they performed creditably in the utility and rescue roles, the latter including the recovery of battle casualties. The potential of the helicopter was clearly demonstrated, therefore, even though the R-4 can be regarded with hindsight as little more than a development type with little useful payload and only indifferent performance.

In many respects similar to the R-4, as indicated by its manufacturer's designation VS-316B, the R-6 was in fact a developed version of the R-4 using the same rotor system and transmission, coupled to a 225hp engine for greater performance, and a more streamlined tadpole-shaped fuselage with a frameless moulded Plexiglas crew cabin for improved fields of vision. The R-6 was built in only modest numbers, but proved invaluable for proving the concept of the helicopter with a high-visibility cockpit enclosure for the aerial observation role.

The defeat of Germany left the USA as the world's most important developer and manufacturer of helicopters after 1945. Other countries, most notably France, the UK and the USSR (now Commonwealth of Independent States), made more or less determined efforts to whittle away the lead built up by the Americans, but in the short term at least, these countries had war-crippled economies and thus needed to start from scratch, which meant that the process would be lengthy. The U.S.A., meanwhile, could step back slightly from pushing new helicopters into large-scale military production in favor of a program that combined far-sighted development with moderate production.

Increasing helicopter performance and payload made it possible in the late 1940s to begin development of helicopters tailored to particular tasks, or with interchangeable equipment to allow any one type to undertake any of several roles when fitted with the right equipment. For example, with the cabin fitted with seats, the larger helicopters could be used for passenger transport: cramped lightweight seating allowed the type's use for military trooping up to the helicopter's payload limit, while more comfortable seating for a smaller number of persons allowed its use for commercial or executive transport. The cabin could be stripped of all such fittings for the carriage of light freight, while the installation of an external hook allowed the carriage of bulky or unwieldy freight, on a line hanging under the fuselage on the center of gravity. Further development in the para-military sphere made it possible for the cabin door to be fitted with a special rescue hoist to allow the type's use in the search-and-rescue role: here the helicopter could hover over the sea or any other inaccessible spot, the weighted rescue sling being sent down to recover one person at a time. In the military sphere, the cabin could be outfitted with mission equipment for a particular task, most notably submarine-detection equipment such as dunking sonar and a tactical plotting system.

This gives some indication of the basic roles that were steadily evolved for the helicopter, and which are now the meat and drink of rotary-wing aircraft operations. In the early days, of course, not all such roles could be considered or undertaken, for the payload of piston-engined helicopters of the 1940s and early 1950s was inadequate for the consideration of any task that demanded the carriage of a heavy load under even moderate climatic conditions, or more than even the lightest load under 'hot and high' conditions: both these circumstances result in reduced air pressure, which degrades the amount of lift that can be generated by the main rotor or rotors, and also reduces the quantity of oxygen available for the engine, resulting in less power for the helicopter's notably power-hungry operating system.

Even in the anti-submarine role, which now uses just a single helicopter to hunt and kill an enemy submarine with a combination of electronic systems and weapons, the helicopters of the early 1950s had to work as two-ship teams, one helicopter carrying the electronics in the hunter role, and the other carrying weapons in the killer role: the hunter detected the target and then called in the killer to finish off the submarine.

During the 10 years after the end of World War II in 1945, considerable strides were made in developing the helicopter in terms of basic practicality, reliability, and payload-carrying capability. Improved understanding of how a helicopter works allowed designers to refine their ideas and so get better performance and payload figures out of a given amount of power. Refinement of structural ideas and the development of new alloys allowed the creation of airframes that were lighter yet stronger, thereby making it possible for the helicopter to carry more payload at higher speed or over greater range. And, of course, engines of greater power were applied to airframes, again increasing payload and performance.

The story of this technical development is well shown by the Sikorsky helicopters of the period: the S-51, S-55 and S-58. The S-51 began life in 1943 as the VS-372, a two-seat observation helicopter for the US Army Air Forces: it was modelled on the VS-316 series and had a similar rotor and transmission, the latter matched to the 450hp Pratt & Whitney R-985 Wasp Junior radial engine. The fuselage was larger and completely new, with considerable internal volume and reverse tricycle landing gear. The type first flew in August 1943 and was designated R-5 (later H-5) or HO3S in US Army Air Force and US Navy service respectively, and was developed in models offering up to 600hp from an R-1340 Wasp radial engine, standard tricycle landing

The Sikorsky S-70 is the type designed to replace the 'Huey,' although for cost reasons it is now supplementing rather than supplanting the older type. This is a highly capable utility and multi-role machine that had been produced in two basic forms as the UH-60 Blackhawk land-based series (illustrated) and the ship-based SH-60 Seahawk and Ocean Hawk series. Of the SH-60 models, the Seahawk is embarked on destroyers and frigates as the Light Airborne Multi-Purpose System Mk III (LAMPS III) helicopter, with equipment for the detection of incoming anti-ship missiles and the discovery and destruction of submarines (magnetic anomaly detector and homing torpedoes). The Ocean Hawk is embarked on aircraft carriers as a dedicated anti-submarine helicopter with dunking sonar and homing torpedoes. There are also electronic warfare, combat rescue, search and rescue, and VIP transport versions in military service, and a utility model in civil operation.

The Eurocopter (Aérospatiale) AS 332 Super Puma series is typical of the modern medium-lift helicopter in that it can be delivered in civil and military forms, the latter in subvariants optimized for land or maritime roles.

gear, and accommodation for three (or pilot and four passengers in the civil S-51). The type was used as an air ambulance, with two external litters, during the Korean War of 1950-53, and was known to the British as the Dragonfly; Sikorsky's UK licensee, Westland, also developed a hybrid type known as the Widgeon with a 520hp Alvis Leonides radial engine, clamshell nose doors and the rotor of the S-55.

The same basic shape was retained in the S-55, which first flew in November 1949. This was designed to carry between eight and 10 passengers, and although retaining the same basic shape as the S-51, introduced quadricycle landing gear and a more angular pod-and-boom fuselage, strengthened by a triangular fillet in the angle between the payload pod and tailboom. The same 600hp R-1340 radi-

Below: The Bell/Boeing V-22 Osprey, seen here in prototype form, presages the advent of a new era in vertical-lift technology. The type is based on the tilt-rotor principle to create a blend of fixed-wing aeroplane and rotary-wing helicopter. This is achieved by the used of two tilting 'proprotor' assemblies on the wing tips: with the shafts of the proprotors swiveled into the vertical position, the V-22 can climb or descend vertically, just like a helicopter, without any need for a runway, but once the machine is airborne the proprotors are tilted forward so that their shafts are horizontal, and the proprotors then serve as propellers with the wings generating lift. The whole concept thus combines the vertical take-off and landing capability of the rotary-wing aeroplane with the higher cruising speeds of the fixed-wing aeroplane.

Another approach to the combination of rotary- and fixed-wing capabilities was represented by the Boeing Vertol Model 76 that first flew in August 1957, with the military designation VZ-2A. This was a tilt-wing research type with one turboprop engine installed in the fuselage and driving, via transmission shafts and gearboxes, two proprotor assemblies mounted on the leading edges of a wing designed to tilt around its spar between the vertical and the horizontal, so that the proprotors generated vertical lift gradually translating into horizontal thrust as the wing was tilted forward.

al and 49ft-diameter main rotor were used, but both payload and performance were increased. About 2,000 were built by Sikorsky and by licensees in France, Japan and the UK: the S-55 served with the American forces as the H-19 Chickasaw, HO4S and HRS, and in British service the type was known as the Whirlwind.

Resulting from a 1952 requirement, the S-58 was planned round a payload of between 16 and 18 passengers, and first flew in March 1954 as a potential replacement for the HO4S in the naval role. A longer fuselage with tailwheel landing gear was adopted, and the new four-blade main rotor was driven by a 1,500hp Wright R-1820 Cyclone radial engine. The type was delivered to the US armed services as the 16-passenger CH-34 Choctaw transport for the US Army, the 12-passenger UH-34 Seahorse assault transport for the US Marine Corps, and as the HSS-1 Seabat submarine hunter or killer for the US Navy, to the British as the Wessex, and to a large number of overseas air arms in a variety of forms. The type also secured useful commercial sales of the 12-passenger S-58B and S-58D variants amongst the overall total of 1,821 S-58s built by Sikorsky. This total was swelled by British and French licensees. British production of the Wessex variant was particularly important, for the British achieved a breakthrough in combining both the hunter and the killer roles in a single airframe, in the process greatly improving the efficiency of helicopter anti-submarine operations.

A similar evolutionary path was followed by the USSR.s premier helicopter designer, Mikhail Mil. First flown in September 1948, the Mi-1 "Hare" was the first major production helicopter of Soviet origin and, powered by a 575hp Ivchyenko AI-26V radial engine, was similar in size and capability to the S-51. Production on a large scale was

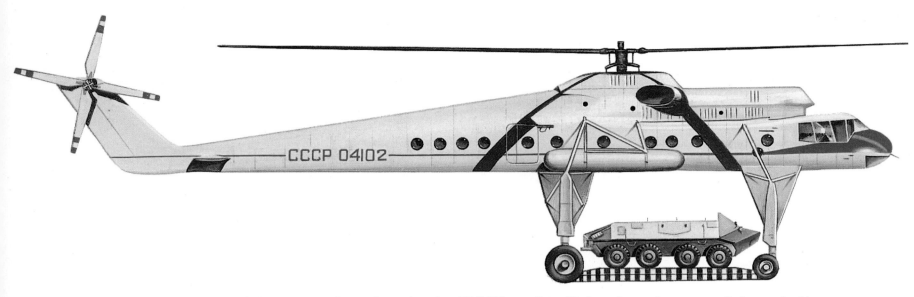

CCCP 04102

Above: Still used in the CIS, the Mil Mi-10 heavy-lift helicopter was an evolution from the Mi-6, from which it inherited its extremely large main rotor powered by two potent turboshafts, but in combination with a comparatively small fuselage, supported by wide-straddling quadricycle landing gear. This last was fitted with attachment for a platform that can be used for the movement of vehicles and other substantial loads.

Below: A classic type still in widespread service, the Sea King was designed in the USA during the 1950s as a twin-turboshaft helicopter for the shipborne anti-submarine role. The British company Westland took the process a step further to produce Sea King improved anti-submarine and airborne early warning helicopters as well as the Commando land-based tactical helicopter.

undertaken in the USSR and in Poland, and many of these helicopters remain in service today. Mil skipped an S-55 equivalent, moving straight to the Mi-4 "Hound" that resembles the S-55 in basic design but the S-58 in size and capability. The Mi-4 is powered by a 1,700hp Shvetsov ASh-82V radial engine, and remains in very widespread service after production in the USSR and China.

By the time the S-58 was in production, a technological breakthrough was about to transform the helicopter. This breakthrough was the adoption of gas turbine propulsion in the form of the turboshaft. Even in its air-cooled radial form without the radiator and water-coollant system of the inline form, the piston engine is a massive item, generally located toward the bottom of the fuselage because of its weight, and therefore driving the high-set gearbox and rotor by means of a long, heavy and space-consuming drive shaft: in Sikorsky helicopters this runs upward and backward at an angle of 45 degrees from the engine in the lower nose to the transmission system above the cabin. By comparison the turboshaft is lighter, more compact and notably free of the vibration associated with the piston engine and, most importantly of all, offers a very considerably higher power-to-weight ratio. This opened up the possibility of higher-powered helicopters with their engine or engines located beside the gearbox in a position above the cabin, which was therefore free of the engine and driveshaft, quieter and, because of the reduced vibration, more comfortable. And quite apart from these improvements, turbine-powered helicopters possess both higher performance and payload than comparable piston-engined helicopters.

The world's first series-built helicopter with turbine powerplant was a French machine, the Sud-Aviation SE 313 Alouette II, that first flew in prototype form in March 1955 with the 530shp Turbomeca Artouste II, after development from the SE 3110 and SE 3120 two-seat prototypes with a 200hp Salmson radial. Performance was improved all round by the turbine powerplant, and the

Alouette II sealed its future success with a world altitude record of 26,932ft The type was later improved as the SA 318C Alouette II Astazou with the more economical 530-p Turbomeca Astazou IIA. The same basic formula was followed with the larger SA 316B Alouette III for seven persons on the 600 shp provided by a derated 870shp Artouste, and by the SA 319B Alouette III Astazou with 600 shp again available, though in this instance from a derated 870-shp Astazou XIV. The Alouette series sold extensively to civil and military operators in many parts of the world, and many remain in service. The same basic concept has been followed by Sud-Aviation's successor, Aérospatiale, in development of other light helicopters such as the SA 315 Lama and Cheetah, the AS 350 Ecureuil and Astar, and the SA 360 and SA 361 Dauphin.

The advantages of the turboshaft were indisputable, and other manufacturers scrambled to cash in on the same change. In the short term, a number of piston-engined designs were revised for turbine powerplants: in the UK Westland developed turbine-engined Whirlwind and Wessex variants, in the USA Sikorsky produced a turbine conversion of the S-58 as the S-58T, and in the USSR Mil reworked the Mi-1 as the Mi-2 "Hoplite" and the Mi-4 as the phenomenally successful Mi-8 "Hip." Both the Soviet helicopters have a twin-turbine powerplant replacing the single radial engine, that of the Mi-2 comprising two 437-shp Isotov GTD-350s and that of the Mi-8 two 1,700shp Isotov TV2-117As.

Coming slightly after the Alouette series, and to date the most widely produced Western helicopter, is the Bell Model 204 series. Bell was already highly successful with its piston-engined Model 47 light helicopter when, in June 1955, it won a US Army competition for its H-40 utility and casualty-evacuation helicopter using a Lycoming T53 turboshaft. Increases in power marked the original HU-1 "Huey" (later UH-1) service helicopters that began to make a name for themselves in the Vietnam War, and steadily improved variants were produced as the large Model 205 and twin-engined Model 212 variants. In its later forms, the series is still in production, and many thousands of the UH-1 series are scheduled to remain in the US Army inventory well into the next century. It is impossible to overstate the importance of the UH-1 series, together with its civil versions: it confirmed the huge value of the utility helicopter in all types of role, and showed that the helicopter was not a useful toy but an essential in the modern world.

The most famous twin-rotor helicopter in the world is undoubtedly the Boeing Vertol CH-47 Chinook, which was developed in the 1960s but is still in gainful production and indeed development. In exterior details the latest Chinooks are little different from their predecessors, but they have vastly improved systems, a modernized rotor system, very much more powerful turboshaft engines and, in its more specialized variants, such as the MH-47 for the use of special forces, an inflight refueling probe, armor, armament, and very sophisticated electronics for very low-level flight under any, and all weather, conditions by day or night.

Above: In both its original French form as Aérospatiale and its current international form as Eurocopter France, this company has designed, developed, produced, marketed and sold a wide assortment of excellent helicopters of all but the largest size, and has achieved equal success in the military and civil fields.

The "Huey" remains the best-known helicopter of that war, but it was partnered by several types that were also very important. At the lighter end of the helicopter scale, the Bell H-13 (military version of the ubiqitous Model 47) was replaced in the observation and scouting roles by the Hughes OH-6 Cayuse and then by the Bell OH-58 Kiowa. These are both excellent machines with high performance and high agility, have secured large markets in their Model 500 and Model 206 civil forms respectively. Further up the size ladder were the medium-lift helicopters. The US forces had started the Vietnam War with piston-engined types such as the twin-rotor Piasecki H-21 Shawnee, but the types that really made a name for themselves were the turbine-powered Boeing Vertol H-47 Chinook and Sikorsky H-53 Sea Stallion. The former is a twin-rotor design derived conceptually from the smaller H-46 Sea Knight assault helicopter of the US Marine Corps, and has gone on to become the West's most important medium-lifter in a number of improved and greatly up-engined variants. The H-53 was designed and introduced with two turbines driving a six-blade main rotor, but this versatile machine has been steadily improved with greater power and, in its latest versions, with three considerably more powerful engines and a seven-blade main rotor. The H-53 series has appeared in specialist forms as an assault transport, flying crane, long-range combat search-and-rescue helicopter, and minesweeper. Both types have a rear loading ramp for access to the large internal hold.

The Vietnam War also witnessed the large-scale development of the armed helicopter. 'Hueys' were frequently fitted with machineguns and rocket-launcher pods, as were the light scout helicopters, but the need to escort troop-carrying helicopters and suppress the ground

The Mil Mi-6, first flown in 1957, was for its time a truly prodigious technical achievement and is still a highly impressive heavy-lift helicopter. With two powerful turboshafts driving an enormous five-blade main rotor, the helicopter can carry an internal load of 65 passengers.

defenses around landing zones demanded the creation of gunship helicopters. The first of these was the amazing AH-1 HueyCobra, essentially a "Huey" with a very narrow fuselage for a gunner and pilot. A chin turret housed a trainable machine gun and/or a grenade launcher, and stub wings carried an assortment of weapons. The AH-1 series is still in development and production in single- and twin-engined forms, with more powerful turret armament and other weapons, suiting it to the ground-attack and anti-tank roles. The latter role also led later to the development of the massive but incredibly impressive McDonnell Douglas Helicopters (originally Hughes) AH-64 Apache, with very advanced electronics, an underfuselage cannon, and the ability to carry up to 16 Hellfire laser-homing missiles under its stub wings.

The USSR has followed a similar path. For trooping and battlefield roles it has the Mi-8 "Hip" and its Mi-17 "Hip" updated version, for medium and heavy lift it has the huge Mi-6 "Hook" that is being supplemented and replaced by the even larger Mi-26 "Halo" as a flying crane it uses the Mi-10 "Harke" whose US counterpart is the rare Sikorsky H-54 Tarhe, for assault transport it operates the Mi-24 'Hind," and for battlefield attack it deploys the Mi-24 "Hind-D," with the Kamov Ka-50 Werewolf "Hokum" and Mi-28 "Havoc" to follow. These are generally comparable with their American counterparts, but are available in larger numbers and generally have a higher payload. This is particularly true of the lift helicopters, which are far more capable than the US machines.

Left: The Boeing Vertol CH-113 Labrador is the Canadian Armed Forces search-and-rescue helicopter. Based on the Model 107 design that was adopted by the US Marine Corps as the CH-46 Sea Knight assault transport helicopter, and also paved the way for the larger model 114 that entered service as the CH-47 Chinook.

The same period has seen a great growth in naval helicopter capability. For the US Navy Kaman and Sikorsky developed the light H-2 Seasprite and medium H-3 Sea King with turbine powerplants. These are both versatile machines with advanced electronics and the ability to carry a substantial warload, and the Sea King has been further developed in the UK by Westland as a more capable naval machine and, as the Commando, a tactical helicopter. The USSR's main naval helicopters are from the Kamov design bureau, which specializes in compact co-axial twin-rotor machines such as the Ka-25 "Hormone" and Ka-27 "Helix." In the UK, Westland has also developed the exceptional Lynx series, which possesses phenomenal performance and agility in both its naval and military versions.

Above: The Boeing Vertol Model 360 is a private-venture technology demonstrator for use in the investigation of the aerodynamics, structures, vibration control characteristics, flight controls, and avionics of a twin-rotor helicopter designed to cruise at 230 mph.

Below: The Sikorsky S-76 is a civil helicopter using much of the technology and aerodynamics developed for the S-70 helicopter that entered military and naval service as the UH-60 and SH-60 respectively. The type has retractable tricycle landing gear and can carry up to 13 passengers.

The tendency in recent years has been toward multi-role civil and military helicopters. For example, the Sea King has civil S-61L non-amphibious and S-61N amphibious variants, which have been widely used in airline and oilrig support operations. Other notable helicopters now available in civil, military and naval versions are the Agusta A 109 from Italy, the Aérospatiale SA 341/2 Gazelle, SA 330 Puma, SA 332 Super Puma and SA 365 Dauphin from France, the MBB BO105 from Germany, and the Sikorsky S-70 from the USA.

The Sikorsky S-70 last serves with the US forces as the UH-60 Black Hawk tactical and SH-60 Seahawk naval helicopters, both of which have been extended from their original applications into a number of specialized variants: the UH-60, for example, has been evolved into unarmed and very heavily armed transport, VIP transport, electronic warfare, combat search-and-rescue and special forces models, while the SH-60 had been developed in parallel into carrier battle group protection, multi-role anti-submarine and missile-targeting, and rescue models.

The future promises to be very exciting for helicopters: the USA is pushing ahead with the Boeing/Sikorsky RAH-66 Comanche (LHX) multi-role military helicopter, and in Europe there are a number of international efforts such as the Anglo-Italian European Helicopter Industries EH.101 and Franco-German Eurocopter types.